**Editorial Project Manager:**
Elizabeth Morris, Ph.D.

**Editor:**
Lynn Gustafson

**Editor in Chief:**
Sharon Coan, M.S. Ed.

**Creative Director:**
Elayne Roberts

**Art Coordinator:**
Cheri Macoubrie Wilson

**Cover Series Design:**
Tina DeLeon Macabitas

**Cover Artist:**
Cheri Macoubrie Wilson

**Product Manager:**
Phil Garcia

**Imaging:**
Ralph Olmedo, Jr.

**Publishers:**
Rachelle Cracchiolo, M.S. Ed.
Mary Dupuy Smith, M.S. Ed.

# INT ACTIVITIES FOR LANGUAGE ARTS

## PRIMARY

**Author:**

Kathleen N. Kopp, M.S. Ed.

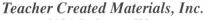

***Teacher Created Materials, Inc.***
6421 Industry Way
Westminster, CA 92683
www.teachercreated.com
**ISBN-1-57690-406-7**
*©1999 Teacher Created Materials, Inc.*
Made in U.S.A.

# TABLE OF CONTENTS

# TABLE OF CONTENTS *(cont.)*

# AN INTRODUCTION TO THE INTERNET

## What Is the Internet?

Much of today's correspondence is done electronically; e-mail, fax, and computer databases send and retrieve information efficiently with the use of a computer. The Internet, commonly referred to as the Net, provides information resources through the use of a network specifically designed for computers. The slice of information from the Internet viewed as text and graphics is called the World Wide Web. Other pieces of the Internet include bulletin board systems, chat rooms, and e-mail services. Internet users can "browse" Web sites for information, order tickets, ask questions of an expert—virtually anything one can imagine—all without having to get out from behind a desk. This information superhighway takes Internet users virtually anywhere they want to go at any time. Travel to Alaska. Want to see the real thing? Book yourself a cruise!

The Internet is nothing more than a network of interconnected electronic data which crisscrosses and zigzags over miles and miles of phone line creating a "web." After identifying a particular topic, one may access Web sites available on the Internet. These Web sites may be independent of one another or connect to related Web pages. Textual "links" are usually a different color than the Web site's normal text. They may be purple or red words embedded on black text, for example. By clicking them, the Web page currently showing connects to the next link. Links can also be graphic items (pictures). Any time the cursor changes to a pointing hand, you know you've found a link.

## How Do I Get There?

In order to explore the Internet, you will need four things:

1. a computer with Internet capabilities,

2. access to a network via a telephone line (an Internet service provider),

3. a Web browser such as *Netscape* or Microsoft *Internet Explorer,* and

4. a destination.

Some online services, such as *America Online* and *Compuserv,* offer a network and Web browser all in one. This means that by launching the Internet icon, users automatically dial in to their network and view the Internet through their browser. Trouble may arise if you live in a remote area where there are no local access numbers to dial. So then not only are you paying the company for the use of their program but you are also paying long distance telephone fees every time you log on. Many smaller (but local) Internet service providers have emerged to save Internet users huge phone bills. Check your local telephone directory and call (yes, with an actual telephone!) to set up access through a local Internet service provider's number. So far, these companies have been rather reasonable with their rates. You usually have a choice of limiting the amount of calling you may do, therefore limiting your Internet exploration time, or signing up for unlimited hours. This might be an option if you are considering downloading information and/or programs off the Internet, which can sometimes take hours, depending on the size of the program. Check out what's available to you in your area, and then decide which method of logging on and browsing is right for you.

# WHAT IS THE INTERNET? *(cont.)*

## So Many Destinations, So Little Time

Once you're safely logged on, the virtual world is at your fingertips! This can be a blessing or a curse. Once you start exploring on the information superhighway, you will find that some roads are endless while others are dead ends. Some are toll roads and others are bridges. Don't be discouraged your first time on the Net. If you make a wrong turn or end up in a deserted town, get back in that vehicle and keep on truckin'!

Take some time to just explore without a destination in mind. Get a feel for how the Web system works. Then try hunting for specific information on a particular subject. A host of popular search engines exist, such as *Excite, Yahoo,* and *Infoseek,* to name a few. Type in a topic of interest and search it. The computer will access any and all sites and related categories that match the topic. You may need to narrow a search by typing in more specific information or broaden a search by typing in a more general subject.

Most search engine home pages list popular subject areas or categories with which to begin a search. Try one of these headings and see where it takes you. If it's not what you're looking for, you can always abort this mission and return to the home page. (An icon specifically for this task, labeled <**Back**>, is at the top of the task bar.)

You've seen the advertisements for a company's Web site or address: http://www.[blah].com. This is called a URL or *Uniform Resource Locator.* Typing in an Internet address or URL at the top of the task bar and striking the return key will launch you directly to that site.

## Can I Ever Get Back?

You may find yourself easily lost if following a site that links and links to related topics. Make a bookmark (click on "bookmark" in the top menu bar and pull the mouse down to "Add this Bookmark") of the site's home page before going on so if you do make a wrong turn but want to keep exploring this site, you won't have to go back ten links to find the original page.

One may presume that no one has ever disappeared while exploring the Internet. It's not the Bermuda Triangle, although it may seem so to new users. A more accurate metaphor is an expanse of quicksand. When you first jump in, you're still fairly safe. But the more you move around, the deeper you get, the more difficult it is to escape. Fortunately, a safety line is always near

# USING THIS BOOK

In this guide is a listing of sites related to specific topics and/or skills which may be part of or supplemental to a primary language arts curriculum. Students will need to access a particular Web site to attain information to complete the activities. Many skill-based activities are related to a particular theme, but are designed to be stand-alone activities as well.

Be sure to access the focus Web site before engaging students in the activity. Web sites tend to change over time, and you don't want to meet with any surprises while browsing live with the class. If for some reason the Web site listed is no longer available, try one of the alternate URLs. Teacher Created Materials attempts to offset this ongoing problem by posting changes of URL's on our Web site. Check our home page at **www.teachercreated.com** for updates on this book.

Many of the focus sites in this guide are actually links of a home page. An arrow or icon at the bottom may indicate "Go Back." If interested, link to view the original site of the focus Web site. But once again, be sure to preview it before doing so with the class.

Read over the steps to become familiar with the students' responsibilities for each task. See "Classroom Management Tips" for more details on how to go about engaging all the students in active Internet learning.

Begin the lesson with the suggested pre-Internet activity. Access the focus Web site, and be prepared to help the students obtain information as they participate in this high-tech manner of research. After the students have completed their online investigation and Internet activity, try one or all of the "Extended Activities" designed to supplement the focus activity.*

Students will need about 20 to 30 minutes to complete the actual online activity. Plan to spend additional time preparing or reviewing with the class during the pre-Internet and extended activities.

The focus Web sites were chosen because of their age-level appropriateness for primary students. Still, some of the textual information may be too difficult for some students to read independently. Students may need assistance when reading the text.

None of the activities calls for visiting a chat group. Chat groups are an instantaneous transfer of typed messages. Since you cannot control what others may write and, thus, what the students may read, this act of information exchange is not recommended. There are plenty of honest, wholesome, kid-related chat groups out there, but this guide is intended to help students use the Internet to gather information, not chat with a stranger.

* Author's Note: The materials list does not include supplies for the extended lessons.

# CLASSROOM MANAGEMENT TIPS

The activities in this guide assume that the students have one computer in their classroom with Internet access. Incorporate the use of the Internet to ensure that all students have equitable experience on the Net in one of several ways. Some of the activities have instructions to launch the focus Web site as a class. Others suggest grouping the students and allowing them to take turns. Regardless of the instructions set forth in the individual activities, make a reasonable choice regarding this organizational strategy to suit the needs of your classroom.

## To launch a URL with the Whole Class

If this is the method of choice or if the activity calls for whole group participation, try attaching an overhead projector or television monitor to the computer if it has these capabilities. This will allow for easier viewing by the entire class. Make sure all the students have a copy of the activity page so they may follow along. Keep everyone on task by rotating volunteers to click at the site and read portions of the information.

## Working in Groups

Another option is to have the students work in small groups to access the desired Web page(s). First provide a whole class lesson demonstrating how to accomplish this. For occasions when you may not be directly available, elicit the help of an adult volunteer to make sure the students are typing in the exact URL, following the directions on the activity sheet, attaining the information necessary for successful completion of the activity, and avoiding the temptation of downloading or e-mailing. Volunteers may be coworkers, parent volunteers, administrators, or perhaps a school media specialist or technology teacher. Even if some students have prior experience using the Internet, be sure to provide them with the support they may need to successfully read the information and complete the activity pages.

One way to manage Internet groups effectively is to have the Internet activity be a center rotation. This way, all the students are engaged in a meaningful project while you help those on the Internet. And all the groups will have a turn on the Internet.

## Save It for Later!

A final option is to save the sites for easier access unless the students are to practice typing in the exact URL. (See "Internet Tips" on page 9 for information about *Web Buddy*, bookmarking, and saving the file.)

# INTERNET TIPS

- Know the exact URL or have a specific topic in mind to investigate.

- Type in the **EXACT** URL (http://). This includes all letters numbers, punctuation, and symbols. Just like an address, sending a package to the wrong door will result in a "return to sender" message or someone else enjoying your visit.

- Typing in a series of words to search will instruct the computer to link all those words individually. Put quotation marks around the words that act as one topic (e.g., "Funny Stories" or "United States Geography").

- Be patient when downloading sites with bountiful graphics as they take up a lot of computer memory. Large graphics may take some time to fully "develop," depending on the speed of the modem and other uncontrollable factors. Try visiting the site and connecting to all the links prior to engaging the class. When you return to the same site within a reasonable amount of time, the computer will have held some graphic information in memory. This will accelerate downloading time.

- Many persons or organizations with Web sites have encouraged businesses to advertise on their page(s). Be on the lookout for links to advertisements and learn to ignore them (unless they are promoting something in which you may have an interest). Teach students to do the same. If you accidentally link to an advertisement, click the <**Back**> arrow at the top of the task bar to return to the previous page.

- Text portions of Web sites usually arrive much quicker than accompanying graphics. Arrow down the page and read the text while the graphics are downloading. Then arrow back up the page and view the artwork and pictures.

- Murphy's Law definitely applies anytime you wish to incorporate technology in the classroom. Expect things to go wrong, even after careful planning. If a Web site is unavailable or your ISP line is busy, have an alternate project ready for the students to complete. If the computer displays a "return to sender" message, double-check to be sure you typed in the exact URL.

# INTERNET TIPS *(cont.)*

- One method of cheating the fickle nature of the Web is to use a Web "whacking" program, such as *Web Buddy*, produced by DataViz. *Web Buddy* will allow you to "whack" or download a single Web page or even an entire Web site, including the links and graphics. It stores the Web pages on your hard drive where they can be accessed with your browser at a later date—even if the page or site has disappeared! Students can enjoy the Web-based activities without the associated wait times during peak Internet hours, or the dreaded "Not Found" error. Teacher Created Materials publishes *Web Buddy*, a book filled with classroom projects and tips on using the *Web Buddy* software which is included on a CD-ROM. It is available for $39.95 by calling (800) 662-4321.

- Another option is to bookmark the sites. (Click <**Bookmark**> from the task bar and drag down to <**Add a Bookmark**>.) When students go online, they only need to click and drag to the correct bookmark; they will automatically be transported to the focus Web site.

- Another way to save sites is by selecting <**File...Save As**>. Choose a drive to save the site and give it an appropriate file name. A word of caution, though. Saving Web sites will only save the text portions (no graphics), and some sites won't save at all. (They look like computer script when the file is opened.) A final option is to simply print the site.

- The information age is here to stay (at least for a while), but some parents may be uncomfortable with their children's availability to the Internet. Before beginning any Internet projects, have parents sign the consent form on page 141.

- Check out **ALL** Web sites before allowing students to go online. Although the Web sites in this guide were consulted beforehand, some sites may have changed, been moved, or somehow incorporated information not appropriate for young students. If this is the case, do some investigative research on your own to find a suitable Web page for the class. Some reliable and user-friendly search engines are listed on the following page.

- Have a question about a site? If the site has FAQ (frequently asked questions), click on the link to see if others have thought the same thing. If your question isn't spotlighted at this link, at least you'll learn information you hadn't thought to ask. E-mail the creator of a site to beg the answers to the most burning questions or express your thanks for providing a most educational Internet opportunity for students. Most creators are quick with their responses; they usually write back by the next day.

---

## To Save Web Sites

- Use the *Web Buddy* program.
- Bookmark the site.
- Save it like a regular document.
- Print it.

---

# SEARCH ENGINES

If you're looking for a particular reading or language arts skill to reference on the World Wide Web, try visiting one of these sites. Type in the topic of interest, whether it be a specific skill or theme, and let the computer do all the work! Once the search engine lists categories and sites related to your search, spend a short while investigating the selections. Chances are the right site is out there just waiting for you to link to it!

**Alta Vista**
http://www.altavista.com/

**Excite**
http://www.excite.com/

**Infoseek Guide**
http://guide.infoseek.com/

**Hotbot**
http://www.hotbot.com

**WebCrawler**
http://www.webcrawler.com

**Yahoo!**
http://www.yahoo.com

**Yahooligans!**
http://www.yahooligans.com
(Yahooligans! is a search engine designed especially for kids.)

# GRAMMAR AND LANGUAGE

Alphabetical Order: Dogs

Antonyms: The Sun

Capitalization: The White House

Color Words: Rainbows

Contractions: Clouds

Months of the Year: Holidays

Parts of Speech: Castles

Punctuation: The Moon

Synonyms: Frogs

# ALPHABETICAL ORDER: DOGS

## Description:
Your class is about to go to the dogs! Students first share what they know about certain breeds and then go online to learn about new breeds.

## Objective(s):
- Identify canine breeds.
- Alphabetize the breeds they chose.

## Materials Needed:
- chalkboard or chart paper
- drawing paper
- 1 copy of page 14 for each student
- 1 white envelope for each student
- large note cards
- 1 copy of the dog head and tail from page 14
- 1 manilla envelope

## To Find a Listing of Dog Breeds on the Web:
Visit the Yahoo! home page at http://www.yahoo.com

Follow the links in this order:

1. **Science**
2. **Biology** or **Life Sciences**
3. **Zoology@**
4. **Animals, Insect, and Pets**
5. **Mammals**
6. **Dogs**
7. **Breeds**
8. Select a breed to view a list of Web sites

## Pre-Internet Activity:
Ask the students what their favorite breeds of dogs are and why. On the board or chart list the breeds along with some features about them. Have the class dog owners share the best part about owning a dog. Then have all the students draw a picture of themselves engaged in an activity either with their own dog or a dog they would like to have (walking him, playing ball, playing Frisbee™, etc.). Allow time for the class to share their pictures. Explain that while they listed several breeds of dogs, there are hundreds more they may never have heard of. The students will go online to learn the names of some different breeds and some information about them, and then use the names of the breeds to practice alphabetizing.

# ALPHABETICAL ORDER: DOGS *(cont.)*

## Teaching the Lesson:

1. Conduct a review lesson about ABC order. Depending on the level of your students, you may determine to which letter (first, second, third, etc.) the students need instruction. Use the list of breeds on the board or chart from the pre-Internet activity for class practice.

2. Distribute a copy of page 14 to each student. Read the directions with the class. Follow the directions on page 12 to view a listing of several dog breeds online. Working in groups of four or five with adult assistance, the students copy down the names of five additional dog breeds (preferably ones they have never heard of before) on the spaces provided. They may link to the breeds to view a list of sites from which they may choose to learn more about each kind of dog.

3. After their online experience, students cut out the doggie head, tail, and six body parts with the breeds listed on them. Give each student an envelope in which to keep their dog pieces. The students practice the skill by placing the pieces in alphabetical order.

4. After everyone has had a turn on the Internet, have each group share the names of the breeds they selected. Write them on large note cards, omitting duplicate breeds. Place them in alphabetical order as a class. Then place the cards and a copy of the doggie head and tail from the student page in a large envelope at a center for students to practice this skill during center time.

## Extended Activities:

1. Have the students work in their ABC order groups to further research one of the dog breeds they listed on their student pages. They make puppets of the dog's face by using paper plates and a craft stick and then use them to give a short presentation to the class about the breed they researched.

2. Invite someone from your local American Kennel Club (AKC) chapter or veterinary clinic to visit the class to share more information about certain breeds. Have the students write a list of questions they would like to ask about dogs in general or specific breeds.

Name _____

# GOING TO THE DOGS!

**Directions:** From the list of dog breeds, select five you know little about. Write the names of the breeds in the spaces below. Cut out all the pieces AND then place them in alphabetical order.

## dachshund

# ANTONYMS: THE SUN

## Description:

It's as simple as night and day! Online sources about the sun allow students to discover adjectives which can be used in antonym pairs.

## Objective(s):

- List adjectives that describe the sun and the moon.

- Identify adjectives which create antonym pairs.

- Write sentences using antonym pairs.

## Materials Needed:

- 1 6" x 9" (15 cm x 22 cm) sheet black construction paper for each student

- 1 6" x 9" (15 cm x 22 cm) sheet white construction paper for each student

- flashlight and globe

- 10 enlarged suns and 10 enlarged moons from page 17

- 1 copy page 17 for each student

- paper plates

- yellow construction paper

## "Sunny" Web Sites to Visit:

**StarChild**
http://heasarc.gsfc.nasa.gov/docs/starchild/
(Click on **Solar System** and then **The Sun**)

**The Sun-A Multimedia Tour**
http://www.astro.uva.nl/michielb/sun/kaft.htm

**The Sun (by Nine Planets)**
http://seds.lpl.arizona.edu/nineplanets/nineplanets/sol.html

**The Sun (from the Night Shadow Home Page)**
http://www.geocities.com/CapeCanaveral/Launchpad/1338/sun.html

# ANTONYMS: THE SUN *(cont.)*

## Pre-Internet Activity:

Distribute a 6 x 9 inch (15cm x 22 cm) sheet of black construction paper and another of white construction paper to each student. Instruct them to draw themselves doing something at night on the black paper and something during the day on the white paper. Students should include a moon in the night picture and a sun in the day picture. Then they glue the two sheets back to back so there is a day picture on one side and a night picture on the other. Sitting in a circle, the students share their pictures. Explain that night and day by are antonyms because they have opposite meanings. Demonstrate how the Earth's rotation causes night and day by using a flashlight and globe. Then tell the students that they will go online to learn more about the sun and practice identifying more antonyms.

## Teaching the Lesson:

1. Conduct a review lesson about antonyms. List the following words on enlarged copies of the sun and moon from the student activity page.

| Write these words on suns: | Write these words on moons: |
|:---:|:---:|
| up | down |
| open | shut |
| forward | backward |
| tall | short |
| inside | outside |
| happy | sad |
| wet | dry |
| summer | winter |
| soft | hard |
| awake | asleep |

Mix up the words and review them with the class. Distribute the shapes to individual students. Instruct students with suns and moons to find their matching antonyms. The class checks to see if all the students found the correct matches.

2. Go online to one of the "sunny" sites listed on page 15 so students may learn more about the sun.

3. Distribute a copy of page 17 to each student. After they complete the page, have them share the sentences they wrote. Write them on chart paper or the chalkboard. Have the students write two of their antonym sentences on a paper plate and decorate it to resemble the sun, using crayons and yellow construction paper. Suspend the plates from the ceiling to spread sunshine each day.

Name _____

# THE SUNNY SIDE OF ANTONYMS

> Remember: Antonyms are words with opposite meanings.

**Directions:** Use six different-colored crayons. Find a pair of antonyms in the suns and moons. Color each matching pair of antonyms a different color. Then, on the back side of this page, choose one pair of antonyms and write two sentences about what you know about the sun, Earth, and moon.

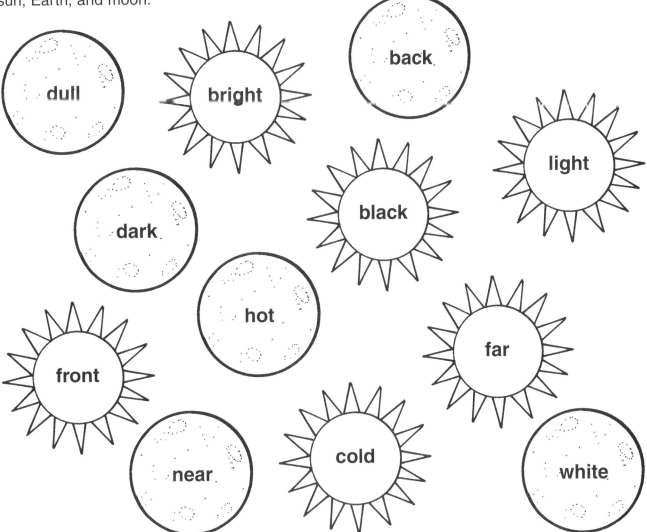

dull

bright

back

light

dark

black

hot

far

front

near

cold

white

# CAPITALIZATION: THE WHITE HOUSE

## Description:

The home of the First Family and all kinds of proper nouns await students on the Internet as they take a virtual tour of the White House.

## Objective(s):

- Define, categorize, and locate proper nouns.

- Practice usage of capital letters on proper nouns.

## Materials Needed:

- chart paper (optional)

- 1 copy of page 20 for each student

## Focus Web Site:

**The White House for Kids**

http://www2.whitehouse.gov/WH/ kids/html/kidshome.html

About this site: Fun facts and valuable information without any political red tape are awaiting students at this Web site. Students follow the first two links to learn about the location of and some history about the White House for use with their online assignment.

## Alternative Web Sites:

**The White House**

http://www.whitehouse.gov/WH/Welcome.html

**The Washington D.C. Fun and Recreation Page**

http://www.his.com/~matson/index.html

## Pre-Internet Activity:

Write the words below on note cards and display them for the class. Ask the students what all the words have in common. *(They all begin with capital letters; they all are associated with Washington D.C., our nation's capital.)* Show the students the location of Washington, D.C., on a U.S. map. Using the map scale, determine the distance from our nation's capital to your home town. Explain that the president lives there in a special mansion called the White House. Then tell the students they will visit the White House on the Internet to learn some more *proper nouns* found there.

| | | |
|---|---|---|
| Pennsylvania Avenue | White House | Washington Monument |
| George Washington | Pentagon | Lincoln Memorial |

# CAPITALIZATION: THE WHITE HOUSE *(cont.)*

## Teaching the Lesson:

1. Conduct a review lesson about proper nouns. Have the students categorize the words from the pre-Internet activity into people, places, and things. Explain that each word begins with a capital letter since it names a special or specific noun. Tell the students that while on the Internet, they should be on the lookout for additional proper nouns.

2. Go online with the class to the focus Web site. Follow links 1 and 2 to read about the location and history of the White House. Write two or three additional proper nouns the class spots from each Web page onto a chart or additional note cards. Review the list and again categorize the words after connecting to all the links.

3. Distribute a copy of the student activity page 20 to each student. Read the directions as a class and have the students complete the page individually. Review the answers as a class after everyone has finished. Have the students tell whether each proper noun names a special person, place, or thing.

4. Tell the class to be on the lookout for additional proper nouns throughout the day. Add them to the list from step 2 above, or begin a "proper noun word wall" wherein you designate an area on one wall to display all the proper nouns the students can find.

## Extended Activities:

1. Have groups of students further research each of the following memorials: Washington Monument, Thomas Jefferson Memorial, Vietnam Veterans Memorial, Arlington National Cemetery, Lincoln Memorial. After discovering the history behind each monument as well as some interesting facts about it, they design a poster to advertise it to attract tourists. Don't forget to capitalize!

2. Using sections of the newspaper, groups of students read about and find proper nouns in articles. They write down all they find on charts, categorized by person, place, or thing.

Name _____

# A PROPER PLACE FOR THE PRESIDENT

**Directions:** Follow links **The Name** and **The White House** at The White House for Kids.
http://www2.whitehouse.gov/WH/kids/html/kidshome.html

As you read, find some proper nouns. Circle each word below that should have a capital letter. The numbers to the right tell how many capitals are missing.

1. The president lives in the white house. (2)

2. The white house is in washington, d.c. (5)

3. The address is 1600 pennsylvania avenue. (2)

4. washington, d.c., is the capital of the united states of america. (6)

5. The pentagon and lincoln memorial are two monuments you can visit. (3)

6. william henry harrison served the shortest term as president. (3)

7. george washington was the person who chose washington as the site of
   our nation's capital. (3)

8. Our second president, john adams, was the first person to live in the
   white house. (4)

9. The white house has also been called the "presidential palace," the "president's
   house," and the "executive mansion." (8)

10. In 1901 theodore roosevelt named the house the white house. (4)

# COLOR WORDS: RAINBOWS

## Description:

Practice reading and applying knowledge of color words is awaiting students on the Internet as they learn about rainbows.

## Objective(s):

- Identify the colors of a rainbow.
- Match a color with its corresponding word.
- Locate objects and then name their colors.
- Write color words.

## Materials Needed:

- enlargement of rainbow on page 22 onto large sheet of bulletin board paper
- note cards labeled with each of the seven color words
- old magazines
- copy of page 23 for each student

## Rainbow Web Sites:

**Rainbows**
http://covis.atmos.uiuc.edu/guide/optics/rainbows/html/rainbow.html

**Rainbow Maker**
http://www.zianet.com/rainbow/homeframe.htm (Click on **The Rainbow Colors.**)

**Questions About Rainbows**
http://www.deltatech.com/rainbowx.html

## Pre-Internet Activity:

Enlarge the rainbow on page 22 onto a large sheet of bulletin board paper. Color each arc in the rainbow, following the example, and write the color words onto plain note cards. Display the rainbow and ask the class to identify it. Then ask them to tell the colors of the rainbow, starting with red at the top. As the students say the color word, secure the note card with the corresponding color word onto its respective arc. Explain that often we combine the last two colors, indigo and violet, into just purple. Next explain to the class that they will have a chance to visit an Internet site that tells all about rainbows. As they read, they should be thinking about objects that come in those colors.

# COLOR WORDS: RAINBOWS *(cont.)*

## Teaching the Lesson:

1. Go online to one of the desired rainbow sites and read about rainbows.

2. Remove the note cards from the enlarged rainbow from the pre-Internet activity and shuffle them. Hold up each card and have students volunteer to place the card on the right color in the arc.

3. As a class, brainstorm two or three items that are the same as the colors of the rainbow. (For simplicity's sake, students may think of things that are purple, not indigo and violet.) Assign each of six groups a color from the rainbow. They hunt through old magazines for items that are their assigned color and glue them to the enlarged rainbow at the front of the room. Display the decorated rainbow in the hallway or on a bulletin board.

4. Distribute a copy of page 23 to each student so they can practice writing and applying their color words.

## Extended Activity:

Play rainbow bingo to further reinforce the students' understanding and recognition of color words. Distribute a plain sheet of paper to each student. They fold the paper four times to make sixteen squares. First they trace on the folded lines. Then the students may color and/or write any of the six color words in all the squares. This is their bingo sheet. Use the cube pattern from page 24 to make a color die. Color and/or write each color word in the squares. Cut and form the cube. Roll the color die. Call out the color that appears on top of the cube. The students may X out any one of the same colors on their bingo sheets.

Continue play until several students have marked four colors in a row. To win a prize of your choosing, they must go to the enlarged rainbow from the pre-Internet activity and identify each of the six (seven) colors represented on it.

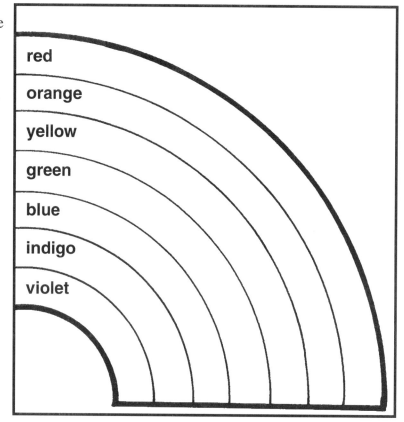

Name _____

# A WORLD OF COLORS

**Directions:** After reading about rainbows on the Internet, trace the color words below. Color the pictures.

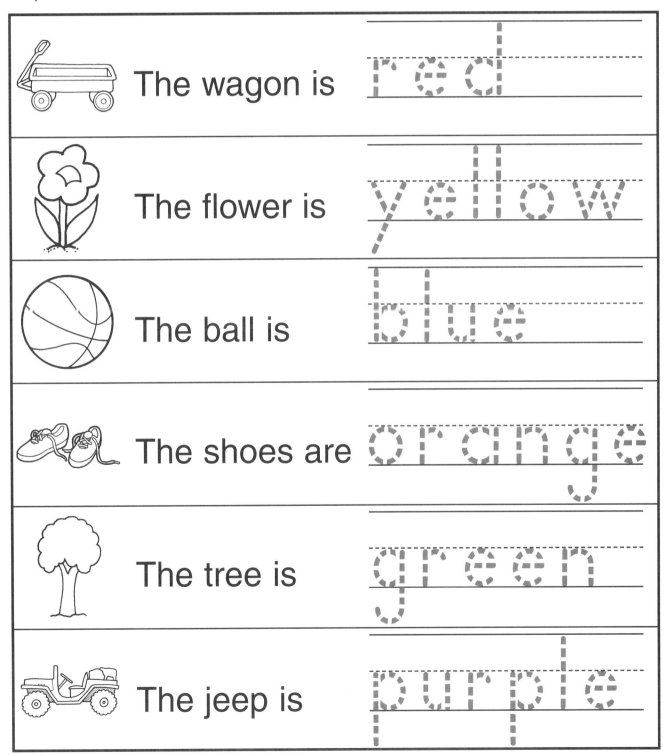

The wagon is    red

The flower is    yellow

The ball is    blue

The shoes are    orange

The tree is    green

The jeep is    purple

Use this cube pattern with the Extended Activity on page 22.

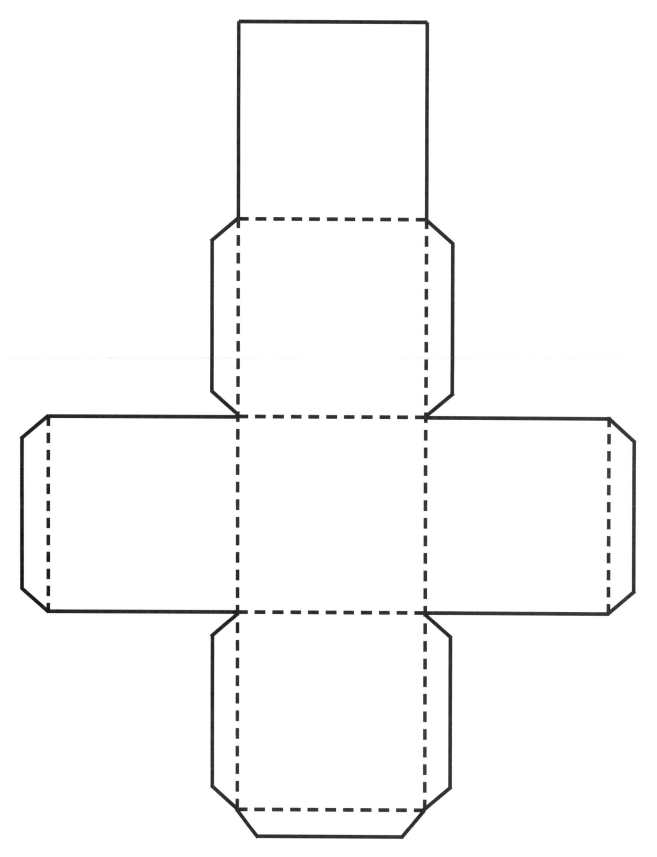

# CONTRACTIONS: CLOUDS

## Description:
Get some swiftly moving contraction action going in your classroom by soaring with a cloud or two.

## Objective(s):
- Identify types of clouds.
- Practice contractions in sentences.

## Materials Needed:
- several pairs 9 x 12 inch (23 cm x 30 cm) sheets of white construction paper
- blank chart paper
- 1 copy of page 27 for each student

## Focus Web Site:
**Cloud Catalog**
http://covis.atmos.uiuc.edu/guide/clouds/html/oldhome.html

About this site: Students' heads will surely be in the clouds once they read about all different kinds of clouds, view pictures of the various formations, and read a detailed account of their classifications.

## Alternative Sites:
**Cloud Page**
http://www.richmond.edu/~ed344/97/weather/clouds.html

**Athena Curriculum Cloud Page**
http://www.athena.ivv.nasa.gov/curric/weather/graphing/clouds.html

**On-line Meteorology Guide**
http://ww2010.atmos.uiuc.edu/(Gh)/guides/mtr/home.rxml

## Pre-Internet Activity:
Take a peek outside at the current weather conditions. If there are clouds in the sky, have the students describe their formations and try to determine whether they are low, middle, or high clouds. If the day is cloudless, have the students describe the different kinds of clouds they have seen in the sky. What are their favorite kinds of clouds to look at? Explain that they will have a chance to learn about all different kinds of cloud formations on the Internet and then practice using contractions.

# CONTRACTIONS: CLOUDS *(cont.)*

## Teaching the Lesson:

1. Holding two sheets of white construction paper together, cut out various cloud shapes.  Cut one of the clouds in half.  Secure the edges of each half to the whole cloud.  Write two words that can be made into contractions on the two outside halves and the contraction they make underneath on the whole cloud.  Use these visual aids to conduct a review lesson about contractions.

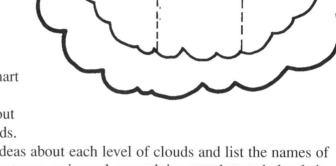

2. Prepare a chart on which the students may keep notes as they read.  Divide a blank chart into three sections: low, middle, and high.  Go online to the focus Web site.  Read about the classifications and descriptions of clouds.  As the students read, they write the main ideas about each level of clouds and list the names of some clouds in each category.  Use this chart as a review when studying weather and clouds in science class.

3. Distribute a copy of page 27 to each student.  Review the directions and allow students time to complete the activity page independently.

## Extended Activity:

Using the contraction clouds from step 1 above, have pairs of students think of an original sentence using the contraction assigned to them.  They write their sentence on a large cloud shape or sentence strip to share with the class.  Ask student volunteers to tell the two words that make up the contraction each pair used.

---

### Sample List of Contractions

| | | |
|---|---|---|
| can't | that's | I've |
| isn't | it's | we've |
| couldn't | she's | you've |
| wasn't | there's | I'd |
| he'll | we're | we'd |
| I'll | they're | he'd |

---

Name _____

# CONTRACTIONS IN THE CLOUDS

**Directions:** After reading about the different cloud formations on the Internet, read the following sentences. Write the contraction for the two words on the line.

1. Fog is a cloud that _____ (is not) in the sky.

   Instead, _____ (it is) on the ground.

2. Most clouds are formed by upward moving air.

   _____ (They are) usually part of a weather system.

3. Cirrus clouds are very high.

   _____ (You will) recognize them by their wispy look.

4. Middle clouds might have light precipitation.

   That means _____ (they will) bring rain or snow.

5. Low clouds are almost always made up of water droplets.

   _____ (Do not) hang around under a low cloud too long.

   _____ (You will) surely get wet!

6. Cumulus clouds are puffy and sometimes look like things we know.

   _____ (Does not) that one look like a clown?

7. Stratus clouds _____ (can not) be good

   news. _____ (They are) so low,

   _____ (it is) sure to rain!

8. Watch out for cumulonimbus clouds! _____ (I would)

   run for cover since they often bring lightning.

# MONTHS OF THE YEAR: HOLIDAYS

## Description:

Each month brings at least one special celebration in the United States. Use these events to encourage students to learn the months of the year in order as well as something about a less well-known holiday.

## Objective(s):

- List the months of the year.
- Identify one holiday in each month.

## Materials Needed:

- twelve 9" x 12" (23 cm x 30 cm) sheets of colorful construction paper
- 1 copy of page 30 for each student

## Holiday Web Sites:

**Holidays on the Net**
http://www.holidays.net/

**Heather's Happy Holidaze Page**
http;//www.heathersholidaze.com/index.html

**U.S. Holidays**
http://shoga.wwa.com/~android7/holidays.htm

## Pre-Internet Activity:

Fold twelve 9" x 12" (23 cm x 30 cm) sheets of colorful construction paper in half. On the outside fold, write the following holidays. Then write the months in which they occur inside the fold. Secure the open edge with a small piece of tape. Review the order of the months of the year. Challenge students to place the holidays in order from January to December. Once all the cards are arranged in order, untape the flap and flip it up to reveal the months. The students check to see if they were correct in placing the holidays in order. Explain that nearly every month in our calendar has many special days and that they will learn more about them on the Internet.

| | | | |
|---|---|---|---|
| January | New Year's Day | July | Independence Day |
| February | Valentine's Day | August | Friendship Day |
| March | St. Patrick's Day | September | Labor Day |
| April | April Fool's Day | October | Halloween |
| May | Mother's Day | November | Thanksgiving |
| June | Father's Day | December | Christmas |

# MONTHS OF THE YEAR: HOLIDAYS *(cont.)*

## Teaching the Lesson:

1.  Now that the students know in which months the holidays take place, can they identify the exact dates on which they occur? Explain that some holidays or memorable dates change from year to year because the exact date falls on different days each year. Use Mother's Day as an example. Since it is celebrated on the second Sunday of May, the date changes from year to year.

2.  Go online to encourage the students to learn more about three of the twelve holidays listed on page 28. Use one of the suggested Web sites as a guide.

3.  Review the months of the year once again. Then allow students to complete page 30.

## Extended Activities:

1.  Divide a large poster into twelve sections. Write the months in order in the boxes. Visit the following Web site to list three to five holidays for each month. Write the holidays in the box with the month in which they occur. Working with a partner or in groups of three, assign each group a month. The groups use electronic and/or traditional means to further research one of the holidays listed on the chart under their designated month. Encourage students to select a holiday they know little about. They write and illustrate information about their holiday on a sheet of paper. Collect the pages from each group and arrange them in order of the months in which they occur. Bind the resulting book and place it in the media center for others to learn about lesser known holidays.

    **Worldwide Holidays and Events**
    http://www.classnet.com/holidays/

2.  Use the former Web site each time you study a country around the world. Select the month in which you are studying that country to discover which holidays people in that country are celebrating. Compare them to U.S. holidays for the same month. Are any holidays the same? Do some further Internet investigative research to find out if they are celebrated the same as well.

Name _____

# EVERY MONTH A HOLIDAY!

**Directions:** Each of the holidays below is listed in order from the beginning of the year to the end of the year. Cut and paste the months in order to show in which month each holiday occurs.

1. [ ]
Dr. Martin Luther
King, Jr.'s Birthday

2. [ ]
President's Day

3. [ ]
St. Patrick's Day

4. [ ]
Earth Day

5. [ ]
Armed Forces Day

6. [ ]
Flag Day

7. [ ]
Independence Day

8. [ ]
Friendship Day

9. [ ]
Grandparents' Day

10. [ ]
Columbus Day

11. [ ]
Veteran's Day

12. [ ]
Christmas

| January | February | March |
|---------|----------|-------|
| April | May | June |
| July | August | September |
| October | November | December |

# PARTS OF SPEECH: CASTLES

## Description:

Castles are architectural marvels which incorporate many purposeful structures within their walls. Students first view the facades and then take a closer look at some finer details as they identify odd nouns that name parts of the castle walls.

## Objective(s):

- Draw and identify parts of a castle.

- Select and write unusual nouns from the Castle Word Bank.

## Materials Needed:

- chalkboard or chart paper

- 1 copy of page 34 for each student

## Focus Web Site:

**Castles on the Web**
http://fox.nstn.ca/~tmonk/castle/castle.html

**About this site:** Take a fantastical adventure back to medieval times as you tour and view castles on the Net. There's even a link for kids that's sure to enhance your unit about castles or the middle ages.

## Alternative Web Site:

**The Castles of Wales**
http://www.castlewales.com/home.html

## Pre-Internet Activity:

Invite one student to come to the chalkboard and draw a castle. Encourage the class to help him out with any details he may leave out. After the castle is finished, ask the students if they can identify any specific parts of the castle (e.g., moat, tower, etc.) List the words on the board or chart and have the students identify them as nouns since they name things. Explain that castles have many more very specific structures on them they will learn about on the Internet.

# PARTS OF SPEECH: CASTLES *(cont.)*

## Teaching the Lesson:

1. Conduct a review lesson about nouns. Write the headings "people," "places," and "things" on the chalkboard. Ask students to think of nouns that deal with castles and/or medieval times. List their responses on the chalkboard or chart.

2. Go online to the focus Web site. Allow the students to tour or view some castles.

3. Distribute a copy of page 34 to each student. Review all the words in the word bank. Explain that any words from the word bank they see in the glossary are nouns since they name a part of (or thing in) the castle. Link to the glossary and begin the search. As students find the words, read the definitions and see if they can identify that part of the castle on the chalkboard.

## Extended Activities:

### Adjectives

Enlarge the dragon on page 33 for use on a bulletin board. Conduct a review lesson about adjectives. As students view the dragon, what words come to mind to describe him? Encourage students to list adjectives not necessarily related to the dragon as well. Have them write their adjectives on white pieces of construction paper cut to resemble puffs of smoke to place on the bulletin board. Entitle it "Adjective Breathing Dragon."

### Verbs

Conduct a review lesson about verbs. What are some actions people living during the middle ages would have done? Working in teams of two or three, have the students write a simple script with a medieval setting. As they perform and act out their skits, the class identifies the verbs acted out. List them on the board or a chart for future reference.

# PARTS OF SPEECH: CASTLES *(cont.)*

## Extended Activities *(cont.)*

**Nouns, Verbs, and Adjectives**

1. Students have a jousting contest with these words as review. Working with a partner, the students make a castle using a small, clean milk carton which has had the top removed. Additional supplies might include brown bags, straws, yarn, craft sticks, dowel rods, etc. Then they write some castle-related nouns, verbs, and adjectives on 2 x 3 inch (5 cm x 8 cm) pieces of construction paper. They place their word cards in the castle (milk carton) and then take turns drawing out a card. The "knight" who draws must identify the word as a noun, verb, or adjective. If correct, he has jousted his opponent and earns one point for himself. If he is incorrect, the card is placed back inside the castle. Then the partner has a turn, and play continues until all the cards have been properly identified. Make a larger castle model from a shoebox. Place additional nouns, verbs, and adjectives inside the box and place it at a center for the students to practice identifying the proper parts of speech.

2. This online review game will have students scrambling to learn their parts of speech! The makers warn it's intended for fourth graders and up, but any students who can think of words to reflect the correct part of speech can play. Simply fill in the proper words and watch your very own "wacky"story come to life!

   **Wacky Web Tales**
   http://www.eduplace.com/tales/

Name _____

# NOUNS IN THE CASTLE

**Directions:** Visit this Web site:

Castles on the Web http://fox.nstn.ca/~tmonk/castle/castle.html

Find six nouns from the word bank below by using the Glossary of Castle Terms link. Write the nouns on the lines in the castle.

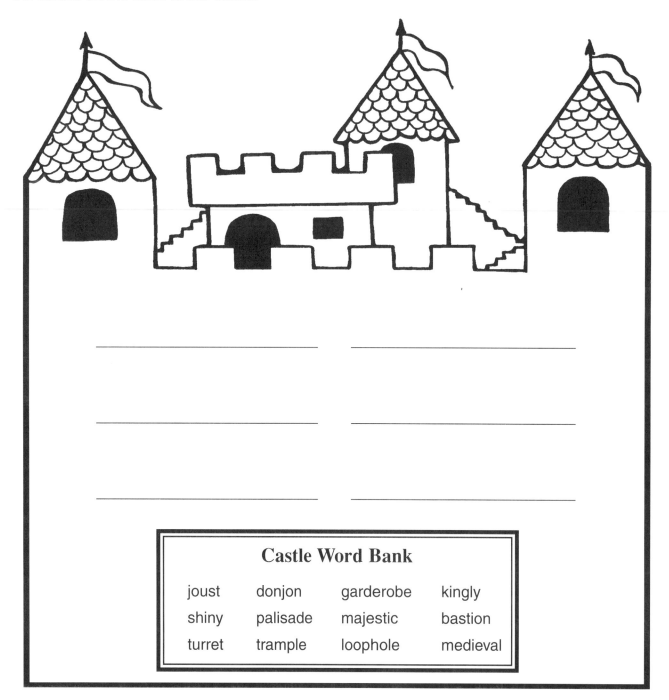

_____     _____

_____     _____

_____     _____

### Castle Word Bank

| joust | donjon | garderobe | kingly |
|-------|--------|-----------|--------|
| shiny | palisade | majestic | bastion |
| turret | trample | loophole | medieval |

# PUNCTUATION: THE MOON

## Description:
Your astronauts will be working overtime to find the correct punctuation marks when they discover more about the moon and the history of lunar travel.

## Objective(s):
- Practice the usage of punctuation marks.
- Read about the moon.

## Materials Needed:
- chalkboard or chart paper
- sentence strips
- 20 copies of the moon on page 36
- 1 copy of page 37 for each student

## Lunar Web Sites:
**Windows to the Universe**
http://www.windows.umich.edu/
(Select **Enter the Site**, then click the **Our Planet** and **Moon** links)

**Nine Planets: The Moon**
http://seds.lpl.arizona.edu/nineplanets/nineplantets/luna.html

**StarChild**
http://heasarc.gsfc.nasa.gov/docs/starchild/ (click on **Solar System** and then **Moon**)

**The Moon**
http://www.hawastoc.org/solar/eng/moon.htm
(click on **Views of the Moon**)

## Pre-Internet Activity:
On the chalkboard or blank chart, have the students recite all they know about the moon. Write their responses in complete sentences, but omit all punctuation. Reread their sentences and ask them to identify what is missing. Fill in the missing marks with a different color of chalk or marker. Explain that although they may know a lot about the moon now, they will learn more on the Internet, and then have a chance to practice using punctuation correctly.

# PUNCTUATION: THE MOON *(cont.)*

## Teaching the Lesson:

1.  Conduct a review lesson about punctuation marks.  Write the following sentences on sentence strips, leaving space where punctuation marks should go.  Make 20 copies of the moon below.  On each moon write the following punctuation marks: 12 commas, 7 periods, and 1 question mark.

    > The Soviets launched the first successful lunar fly-by on Jan 2 1959
    > Did you know Mr Yuri Gagarin was the first man in space
    > There are many space centers across the U S
    > One is in Houston Tex
    > Apollo missions 7 8 9 10 11 12 13 14 15 16 and 17 were all manned

2.  Post the sentence strips for the students to read and then help them decide which punctuation marks are missing.  Allow student volunteers to secure the correct moons in the correct locations on the sentences.

3.  Visit one of the suggested lunar Web sites from page 35.  As the class reads, they add new information they learn to their narration from the pre-Internet activity.  They should include correct punctuation marks where needed.

4.  Distribute a copy of page 37 to each student to complete independently. Review the answers, if desired, when complete.  Students should explain why each punctuation mark is necessary.  Which rules of grammar does each mark follow?

## Extended Activities:

1.  Neil Armstrong's first steps on the moon in 1969 would compare to a present-day astronaut's first steps on Mars.  Have the students write a possible dialog among the three *Apollo 11* astronauts (Edwin "Buzz" Aldrin and Michael Collins were the others) as they prepare to take those first "giant steps." Use this activity to introduce or reinforce quotation marks.

2.  Create a data chart of the nine planets and the number of moons each planet has. Have the students use electronic and/or traditional means to further investigate some of the more notable moons in our solar system.

Name _____

# DIGGING UP CRATERS

**Directions:** Every punctuation mark from the paragraphs below has fallen into a lunar crater! Help rescue the correct marks by writing them where they belong. The stars tell how many marks are missing in each row.

⭐1 Did you know that the Moon is about one-fourth the size of the earth  That

⭐1 means about four moons could fit inside one earth  The moon also has less

⭐2 gravity—one-sixth to be exact  That means if you jump one foot on earth you

⭐1 could jump six feet on the moon

⭐3 The moon also has no wind atmosphere weather or magnetic field as we have

⭐3 here on earth  But like the earth the moon does not give off its own light  It

⭐4 reflects the sun s light like a mirror  The dark regions or *maria* that we see are

⭐2 smooth parts of the moon  The lighter regions are hilly crater-filled parts of the

⭐1 moon

⭐1 Astronauts had spent a lot of time trying to get to the moon  The Soviets actually

⭐6 launched the first man in space on Apr 12 1961 On July 20 1969 Mr Neil

⭐1 Armstrong of the United States was the first person to set foot on the moon

Check your work! Write how many of each punctuation mark you wrote.

_____ commas _____ periods _____ exclamation marks

_____ question marks _____ apostrophes

# SYNONYMS: FROGS

## Description:
Students will "hop" right into learning about synonyms with these reinforcing activities centered around the topic of frogs.*

## Objective(s):
- Brainstorm frog related words.
- Identify synonyms.
- Practice using synonyms in sentences.

## Materials Needed:
- chart paper
- fly swatter (optional)
- 1 copy of page 40 for each student
- several copies of the frog and lily pad patterns below

## Frog-related Web Sites:
**The Froggy Page**
http://frog.simplenet.com/froggy/

**Frogland**
http://www.teleport.com/~dstroy/index.html

## Pre-Internet Activity:
Have the students brainstorm everything they know about frogs. Record their responses in a pond drawn on chart paper. Review the list at the end of the brainstorming session. If the class thinks the statement is true, they jump like a frog once. If they disagree with the statement or think it is false, they make a croaking sound. Explain that they will have a chance to learn more about frogs on the Internet as well as practice identifying synonyms.

*\* See "Thematic Poetry" on page 91.*

# SYNONYMS: FROGS *(cont.)*

## Teaching the Lesson:

1. Play this synonym review game. Using the list of synonyms below or some of your own, call out a pair of words. Since the words are synonyms, the students hop like frogs to someone else's seat. Include in the called-out words pairs that are not synonyms. When non-synonym pairs of words are called, the students simply "gribbet" like a frog and wait for a synonym pair to be called so they may hop along to the next desk.

2. Go online to learn more about frogs at one of the suggested Web sites listed on page 38. Since frogs are known to like flies, hand a fly swatter to one student to come to the computer to click and explore. After connecting to a few links, he hands the swatter to another student who may do the same, and so on.

3. Distribute a copy of page 40 to each student to complete independently.

4. Label the frog and lily pad patterns on page 38 with the synonym pairs below for students to practice during center time.

## Extended Activity:

Post the list of synonyms for the students to see. Working with partners, they devise a short script about frogs, using one of the synonym pairs. First, they should consider the characters of their skits. They can pretend to be frogs, two friends talking about frogs, scientists studying frogs, high school students dissecting frogs, etc. Then they should consider their settings: the pond, aquarium, lab, school, etc. Finally, they write their two-synonym skits keeping their characters and settings in mind. After the partners perform for the class, the class members should identify who they were, where the skit took place, and the two synonyms they included.

### Sample Synonyms

| | | | | | |
|---|---|---|---|---|---|
| ill | sick | harm | damage | fat | chubby |
| fast | quick | close | shut | sly | clever |
| exit | leave | buy | purchase | smell | odor |
| easy | simple | walk | step | old | aged |
| hard | difficult | hop | jump | stare | gaze |
| right | correct | big | large | happy | glad |
| funny | amusing | cozy | comfortable | smart | wise |

Name _____

# A POND FULL OF SYNONYMS

Directions: After reading about frogs on the Internet, read these sentences. Find a word that means nearly the same as the word in parentheses. Write the synonym for each word on the line.

1. Frogs can _____ really far.
   (hop)

2. Some frogs have a terrible _____.
   (smell)

3. Frogs seem to _____ for a long time without blinking.
   (stare)

4. The frog in the pet store is quite _____.
   (fat)

5. No one would want to _____ him because he eats too much!
   (buy)

6. My friend has a pet frog that is quite _____.
   (aged)

7. Once he got loose, and we had to _____ for him.
   (seek)

8. He was in a _____ closet.
   (shut)

9. Do you think he was trying to make a _____ getaway?
   (quick)

10. Handling frogs makes me _____ to my stomach!
    (ill)

## Frog Synonym Word Bank

| | |
|---|---|
| sick | old |
| chubby | search |
| jump | gaze |
| closed | fast |
| purchase | odor |

# WRITING

Biographies

Developing Sentences

Electronic Mail

Electronic Postcards

Newspaper Stories

Original Stories

# BIOGRAPHIES

## Description:

Students put their inquisitive minds to work, first reading about famous authors and then writing a biography about someone they know.

## Objective(s):

- Read about two authors.

- Identify interesting information found in biographies.

- Develop questions for writing a biography.

- Write a biography.

## Materials Needed:

- 1 copy of page 45 for each student

- drawing paper or copy paper

## Focus Web Sites:

**Biography (from Encyclopedia Britannica)**
http://www.biography.com/

**About this site:** Here you'll find concise entries of famous people. Select the option to search and then click the letter of the last name of the person you wish to reference.

**Biography Maker**
http://www.bham.wednet.edu/bio/biomaker.htm

**About this site:** This site offers readers clear, simple directions on how to go about writing a biography. Students follow a four-step process and then can compare their work against the six traits of effective writing. This site is written assuming the students will write about a famous person to research; this activity calls for students to decide on any about whose life they would like to find out more.

## Pre-Internet Activity:

Randomly assign each student a partner. Explain that they will have five minutes to learn about each other, then they will introduce their partner to the class, pretending he or she is a new student. Allow time for the students to complete this activity. Explain that if they were to write down all the information they learned, they would have written a biography, a true story about someone's life.

# BIOGRAPHIES *(cont.)*

## Teaching the Lesson:

1. Now that the students have heard each other's biographies, go online to the first focus Web site to read biographies about two famous authors, Beatrix Potter and Dr. Seuss. Discuss the information that was presented in each biography and make a listing of it on a chart. Help the students compare the kinds of information included in the authors' biographies and the students' biographies. Which seem more interesting? Why?

2. Next visit the second focus Web site. Follow the links to read the directions for writing a good biography. Did the students follow each of the four steps during the pre-Internet activity? Why do they think the author of this site thinks each of these steps is important?

3. Distribute a copy of page 45 to each student. First have the students decide on a person about whom to write a biography. (See options below.) Next discuss appropriate questioning techniques. Explain how a question they ask might actually be a statement that begins "Tell me about...." They should avoid asking questions that begin with "do" and "is" which usually evoke a "yes/no" answer. Students may use the ideas at the **Questioning** link for more help.

   **Option 1:** If allowing the students to choose a person about whom to write a biography, instruct the class to give their ideas serious consideration. They may elect to interview a brother, uncle, friend, or relative who lives far away. Students may make a flip book or 8-page book from one sheet of paper after completing the "synthesis" phase of their assignment. (See directions on page 44.)

   **Option 2:** You may wish to have the students complete this activity with the same partners they had during the pre-Internet activity, or you can compile a list of volunteers from around the school building about whom the students may write a biography. The resulting biographies could then be bound to create a biography anthology about the class to place in the reading corner or about school personnel to place at the front office for visitors to enjoy.

# BIOGRAPHIES *(cont.)*

## Extended Activities:

1. If following option 1 from "Teaching the Lesson," schedule times throughout the week when the students may bring to school the person or pictures of the person about whom they wrote. Nothing is more motivating than live show and tell!

   If following option 2, have the students share their biographies when the student they wrote about is "person of the week." Allow each honored student to bring in a special stuffed animal or other item from home to complement his or her biography. Or invite each staff member to the room to share their biographies during a designated time.

   With either option, the class can see the real person and ask questions that may not have been answered in the students' writing. This is also a great time to celebrate everyone's unique lives!

2. Discuss the meaning of an autobiography. Bring in a decorated box filled with items that describe you (e.g., special awards, books, cooking utensils, weights, beach towel, wrench, or any items you use during your free time). Demonstrate how to follow the same guidelines to write an autobiography about yourself. Discuss whether the students would prefer writing an autobiography or having someone else write a biography about them. Why? What are the advantages and disadvantages to each?

**Directions for making a flip book:**
Fold the first of three sheets of 8½ x 11 inch (22cm x 28 cm) copy paper 2 inches from the top. Fold the second sheet 3½ inches (9.3 cm) from the top and the third sheet 5 inches from the top. Insert each page to make a six-page flip booklet. The top sheet may act as the title page. (With four sheets, fold at the 2, 3, 4, and 5-inch marks.)

**Directions for making an eight-page book from one sheet of paper:**
Fold a sheet of 9 x 12 inch (23 cm x 30 cm) drawing paper in half three times. Open the second and third folds and cut a slit starting at the center of the first fold and stopping at the mark of the third fold.

On a horizontal edge of the paper, stand the paper up. The slit in the paper will be horizontal too. Fold the paper back so the slit is now on top. Push the edges of the paper toward the center, forming a square-like opening in the center. Continue pushing to the center to get a cross-like shape from your paper. Fold the paper to have four double-sided pages.

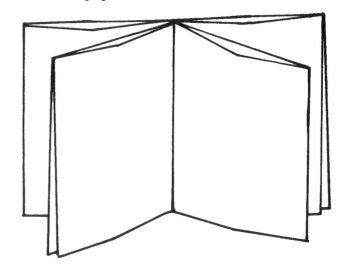

Name _____

# THE MAKING OF A BIOGRAPHY

**Directions:** Decide on a person about whom to write a biography. Write his or her name on the top line. Decide on four questions you will ask this person. Try to think of interesting questions that will require more than a "yes" or "no" answer. Use additional paper, if needed.

**My biography about** _____

Date of birth _____ Place of birth _____

**Questions I will ask:**

1. _____

   Answer: _____

   _____

   _____

2. _____

   Answer: _____

   _____

   _____

3. _____

   Answer: _____

   _____

   _____

4. _____

   Answer _____

   _____

   _____

   _____

After the interview, use the information you learned to write a biography about your person.

# DEVELOPING SENTENCES

## Description:
Students go online to learn about bears and choose words about bears which will create descriptive sentences.

## Objective(s):
- Illustrate a simple sentence about bears.
- Discuss the varied pictures drawn by the class.
- Examine methods to create specific details in sentences.

## Materials Needed:
- large sheet of drawing paper for each student

## Bear-Related Web Sites:

### The Cub Den Homepage
http://www.nature-net.com/bears/cubden.html

This site has plenty of bear information directed towards young learners. Students may read about bears or select one of several interest group articles.

### The Bear Den (by Bear TAG)
http://www.bearden.org/

Choose any one of several category links for information, games, and facts about bears.

### Bears.org
http://www.bears.org/

Chose any one of several category links to read up on various species of bears, bear myths, essays, and bear-related media.

### North American Bear Center
http://www.bear.org/

This site offers information about black bears in North America as well as facts and information about bears in general.

# DEVELOPING SENTENCES *(cont.)*

## Pre-Internet Activity:

Write this sentence on the chalkboard:

## The bear sat.

Distribute a sheet of large drawing paper to the students and ask them to draw an illustration for that sentence on one half of the paper. Students will probably have questions about the details of the drawing. Simply repeat the assignment, giving no further details. Afterwards, have the class share their drawings. Ask why different people seem to have drawn different bears in different environments. Did any one person draw the bear correctly? Why or why not? Explain that when writing sentences, it's important to give clear, specific details so that the reader may interpret the writer's meaning clearly.

## Teaching the Lesson:

1. Collect the students' drawings for later use. Go online to one of the bear sites listed on page 46 so the students may learn more about bears. Write some facts and information from the site onto an enlargement of the bear on page 46 for the students to refer to later.

2. Review the sentence, "The bear sat." Ask the students to elaborate on the sentence by using some of the information they learned at the Web site. When they finish, the sentence may look something like this:

> The large black bear with one ear sat on a
> rock in the forest near the stream.

3. Redistribute the students' drawings from the pre-Internet activity. On the second half of the paper, they illustrate the new and improved sentence. Allow time for the class to share their drawings once more. What do they notice has changed since they illustrated the first sentence?

## Extended Activity:

Write several nouns and verbs on separate cards. Place the nouns in a brown bag marked nouns and the verbs in a brown bag marked verbs. Have pairs of students select one noun and one verb from each bag and form a sentence. Then they elaborate the sentence to make it more specific and illustrate it on a small sheet of construction paper.

# ELECTRONIC MAIL

## Description:

Writing letters has certainly changed since the advent of e-mail. No longer are we tied to those stuffy letter formats. However, students must be aware that the content of an e-mail message should still be taken seriously.

## Objective(s):

- Discuss the variety of formats in letters.
- Compose e-mail messages.
- Practice letter writing.

## Materials Needed:

- examples of friendly and business letter formats (see page 49)
- 1 copy of page 50 for each student

## Places to E-mail

**Bill Nye the Science Guy**
http://www.disney.com/DisneyTelevision/BillNye/

Try the experiment of the day, or simply e-mail Bill Nye with a question or comment. (Select the e-mail link.)

**Seussville**
http://www.randomhouse.com/seussville

This site is perfect for younger students since the questions are pre-composed. Choose one of the available inquiries to ask Cat in the Hat. Submit your e-mail address to receive a prompt response.

**Cyber-Seuss**
http://www.afn.org/~afn15301/drseuss.html

Older primary-aged students may prefer to e-mail the creator of this site after linking to any of the multitude of pages with information and games about Dr. Seuss and his writings.

**Goosebumps Official Site**
http://place.scholastic.com/goosebumps/index.htm

Students may write to Scholastic with questions or comments about this popular series of books. Included at the site are several Goosebump-related links sure to get the cobwebs scooped out of the class' skulls!

## Pre-Internet Activity:

Ask the students if they have ever received a letter in the mail. Who wrote to them? Why? Have the class brainstorm different reasons people write letters (e.g., *to inform, conduct research, complain, compliment, inquire, send thanks, make a request, send a friendly note, and many others*). Explain that the purpose of the letter dictates how formal it is. When writing to a company, the letter must follow a more businesslike format; letters to friends follow a friendly letter format. Review and compare the parts of a friendly letter and business letter with the class.

# ELECTRONIC MAIL *(cont.)*

## Parts of a Friendly Letter

Heading:                     return address

                                     date

Greeting: Dear John,

Body:      Write your friendly letter here. Your letter should tell happy events that are happening to you as well as ask your friend questions so he or she may respond.

Closing:      Your friend,

Signature:      your name

## Parts of a Business Letter

Heading:                     return address

                                     date

                          Mr. Jones

Inside Address: 123 Business Lane

                          Any Town, State 12345

Greeting:      Dear Mr. Jones:

Body:      Write your business letter here. State your purpose. Be brief.

     Don't forget to thank this person for his or her time.

Closing:      Sincerely,

Signature:      name written

                  name typed

## Teaching the Lesson:

1. Explain that electronic mail (or e-mail) is a great way to use the computer to communicate with another person. Because of the way it formats return addresses, the letters written using e-mail are a lot less formal than paper and pencil letters. Usually, people omit the heading since the receiver automatically sees who sent the letter as well as the date and time it was sent. So all the students need to consider is the purpose and content of the letter they will send.

2. Distribute a copy of the activity sheet on page 50 to help students determine the purpose of each e-mail message.

3. Go online as a class to one of the sites listed on page 48. Aside from the Seussville site, students may practice writing letters via e-mail. Before composing their messages, they should consider the purposes of their letters as well as edit them for content.

Name _____

# I'VE GOT E-MAIL!

**Directions:** Read each electronic message below. Answer the questions and then decide whether its purpose was friendly or business.

---

**Subject: Lost tooth**

**Date:** Fri, 23 Mar 1997 4:23:21 p.m. EST

**From:** Jeffy <jjplease@littletykes.net>

**To:** Grandma <nbkomb@essex.com>

Dear Grandma,

I lost my first tooth! The tooth fairy is coming tonight. Mom says she gives money for lost teeth. I will be rich!

Love,

Jeffy

---

To whom did Jeffy send an electronic message? _____

What is Jeffy's return e-mail address?

_____

Was this e-mail friendly or business?

_____

---

**Subject: Cool toy**

**Date:** Wed, 12 Jan 1998 3:15:15 p.m. EST

**From:** Jack <jrstop@myhouse.net>

**To:** Little Toy Company <toys@littletoy.com>

Dear Little Toy Company:

I got one of your Super Sonic Soakers for Christmas. It was really neat to watch the water shoot across the living room at my little brother! But the trigger broke the second time I used it. I think maybe my brother chewed it off, but Mom says he couldn't have done that without getting sick. We returned it to the store and got a new one that works even better!

Thank you for making such a neat toy.

Sincerely,

Jack

---

On what date did Jack send his message? _____

What was he writing about?

_____

_____

To which company did he write?

_____

What was its e-mail address?

_____

Was this e-mail friendly or business?

_____

---

# ELECTRONIC POSTCARDS

## Description:

Everyone enjoys receiving a friendly note when he or she least expects it. Here's a chance for your students to share some happy thoughts via cyberspace!

## Objective(s):

- Discuss the reasons people send cards to each other.
- Compose a postcard on the World Wide Web.

## Materials Needed:

- postcards to share (See parent letter, p. 53)
- 1 copy of the blank postcard on page 53 for each student
- 5 x 8 inch (13 cm x 20 cm) note card for each student
- 1 copy of the e-mail letter on page 98

## Electronic Postcard Web Sites:

### Blue Mountain Arts
http://www.bluemountainarts.com/

This user-friendly site focuses on sending a "happygram" related to the most recent holidays. The graphics are cute and inviting, and messages are easily retrieved.

### Awesome Cyber Greeting Cards
http://www.marlo.com/card.htm

This site is a little more complicated than the former but offers a wide variety of greetings spanning a multitude of topics. Users are also allowed to include that "personal touch" not available from Blue Mountain.

### The Electronic Postcard
http://postcards.www.media.mit.edu/Postcards/

Here students can select from a wide variety of drawings and artwork. Simply choose the image, write the message, and mail it!

### Kids Cards
http://cards.creativekids.com/

Students will enjoy this child-centered site, but the options are quite limited and may not suit your card's needs.

### Send an Alien
http://anyhost.simplenet.com/bag-o-aliens/send/index.html

Here's a message a friend or relative definitely was not expecting! Unfortunately, there is no option to view the card (or the alien) before sending it. You'll just have to send one to yourself to see what it looks like!

# ELECTRONIC POSTCARDS *(cont.)*

## Pre-Internet Activity:

Have the students bring a postcard from home that they or their family have received in the mail, or ask parents ahead of time to purchase and donate a suitable postcard from the store. (See page 53.) Display all the cards and ask the students to tell about a time when they have either received or sent a postcard to a friend or relative. What was the message? How long was it? How did they feel either as the sender or receiver? Explain that people send postcards to let others know they are thinking about them without having to sit down and write a complete letter. It's a convenient way of communicating by mail. Next explain that the students will have a chance to send a postcard to a friend or relative on the Internet, using a site that offers this service free!

## Teaching the Lesson:

1. Discuss the reasons people send letters, cards, and postcards to each other. (See pages 48 to 49 for a more detailed lesson.) Explain that since postcards usually have limited writing space, the message must be brief but thorough.

2. Have each student first think of someone to whom they would like to send a postcard, whether they have Internet access or not. Then they consider the purpose of the correspondence (friendly, holiday greeting, thank you, etc.) and plan a short message to that person. The planning card on page 53 may help students to plan. After they finish writing, they glue it to a 5 x 7 inch (13cm x 18 cm) note card and decorate the blank side accordingly.

3. For students with friends or relatives with Internet access, provide the permission slip on page 98. Students who do not know anyone with e-mail may partner up with someone who does to share in the electronic postcard experience.

4. Decide ahead of time which electronic postcard site you think is best for your students' notes. Allow them to access the site and follow the directions to electronically send their messages.

5. After a few days, invite students to share whether they received responses from their e-mail recipients.

Dear Parents:

We will soon be discussing postcards and correspondence skills. Please call or write to a friend or relative and ask him or her to send your child a postcard through the mail, or simply help by purchasing a postcard from the store and sending it to school with your child. All postcards will be returned. We need them before

(date)_____.

Thank you for your support!

Sincerely,

Parents
Any Address
Hometown, ST
11111

_____,

_____

_____

_____

_____

_____,

_____

_____

_____

_____

# NEWSPAPER STORIES

## Description:

Extra, Extra! Students consider the importance of newsworthy events and then act as roving reporters when they report a news story to the class.

## Objective(s):

- Name and list attributes of a newsworthy event.
- Select a news story from the Internet.
- Summarize a news story for the class.

## Materials Needed:

- news article of student interest from local paper
- 1 copy of page 57 for use as a class
- 1 copy of page 57 for each pair of students
- bulletin board entitled, "Get Your Nose in the News"
- enlarged artwork on page 56 for bulletin board

## Newsworthy Web Sites:

**Children's Express**
http://www.ce.org/

Some articles may be directed towards older students, but the stories are also newsworthy for primary aged students. This site allows students to write an editorial or story of their own for publication, answer polls, and give feedback; this is a very interactive news site students of all ages will enjoy!

**Kid News**
http://www.yakscorner.com/Kidnews/

Here students may select a news category and then choose a title of an article that piques their interest. All the articles have been written and submitted by students of varying ages. There is also for teachers a note explaining how to go about publishing students' writing on the Web.

**Tomorrow's Morning**
http://www.morning.com/index.html

This publication offers viewers a chance to experience child-centered news articles on the 'Net. Click **Current Issue** to read the latest kid-related news stories.

**Yak's Corner**
http://www.yakscorner.com/

Here's just the right online news magazine to motivate students to pay attention to current events. Click **Kid News** to see a list of articles of interest to young learners.

# NEWSPAPER STORIES *(cont.)*

## Pre-Internet Activity:

Hunt a late-edition newspaper for a suitable story of interest to students. (Ideal articles might be about events happening in your area or those related to current movies or celebrities.) Ask the students to tell about some current events they have heard on the news. Ask them why they think those stories were newsworthy. Then read the article you have selected to the class. While reading, complete a copy of page 57 together. Ask the students to once again consider why this story was important enough to be featured in the local paper. Explain that the students will get to go online to read a news story of their choosing and give an on-the-spot feature report to the class.

## Teaching the Lesson:

1. Have the students consider the news stories they shared during the pre-Internet activity. As a class, make a list of story attributes and/or types of articles that the students consider important and would motivate them to read the story.

2. Working in pairs or groups of three, have the students log on to one of the Web sites listed on page 54, select a news story of interest, and complete a copy of page 57.

3. After writing their summary, the students act as news reporters to give an in-depth report to the class. Provide them with a microphone and any other props they feel are necessary to take the class "on location" to the featured news site.

4. Post the students' worksheets on a bulletin board entitled, "Get Your Nose in the News!" (See page 56).

## Extended Activities:

1. Ask the students to consider important, late-breaking news that might be happening in their very own school. Working in pairs, have the students go "on the hunt" for fascinating news stories around the school. Send one pair at a time to visit previous teachers, cafeteria workers, secretaries, librarian, administrators, or any other school personnel to probe for a story. Students may use the news guide on page 57 to organize their information and write an original summary or news article. Then they word-process their writing. Collect all the pairs' work and cut and paste the articles onto a sheet of butcher paper measuring 14 x 56 inches (35 cm x 40 cm) folded to measure 14 x 28 inches (35 cm x 140 cm) to resemble a real-life newspaper. Include a catchy title (*The Worthington World News, Forest Elementary Express,* etc.) at the top of the paper, date it, and place it in the reading corner for all students to enjoy during free reading time.

# NEWSPAPER STORIES *(cont.)*

## Extended Activities *(cont.)*

2. Just as an interesting book title might pique students' attention, so does an article's title, or headline, grab a newspaper reader's attention. Have each student copy down the title of one newspaper story from home to share. (Supply papers in class for those who don't receive the daily paper.) After the students have shared their headlines, ask them to consider how they were written. Are there complete sentences? What exciting words draw the reader to want to read that article? What else do they notice about the headlines? How are they different from book titles? After discussion, have the students create an original headline using the letters of their name as the first letter of each word. (They may insert words like *a, an, the,* and *and* where needed.) Then they write an original news story to accompany the headline.

> Example:  Someone
>
> Captures
>
> Octopus in
>
> Terrified
>
> Town

3. Students will be up to date on current events when you share some real world news. Visit this Web site once each week with the class to keep them current on world events.

**Time for Kids**
http://pathfinder.com/TFK/index.html

**U.S. News Online**
http://www.usnews.com/usnews/home.htm

Enlarge this graphic to use on bulletin board, "Get Your Nose in the News."

Name _____

# NEWSWORTHY EVENTS

**Directions:** Log on to an Internet news site assigned by your teacher. Select a feature story and complete this outline of the news report.

Title of article _____

What the event was _____

Who was featured _____

Where it took place _____

When it took place _____

How this event affected others _____

Now use this outline to summarize the story. Report the events to the class.

_____

_____

_____

_____

_____

_____

_____

_____

# ORIGINAL STORIES

## Description:
Students often write imaginative stories. Here is a chance for your class to read what other students across the United States and Canada have written.

## Objective(s):
- Select and read a favorite journal story to the class.
- View students' stories online.
- List qualities of appealing stories.

## Materials Needed:
- writing journals (optional)
- writing paper
- 1 copy of the permission slip on page 98 for each student

## To Access Students' Stories on the Internet:
1. Go to the Yahooligans! home page at http://www.yahooligans.com
2. Click the School Bell link.
3. Click the Elementary Schools link.
4. Search for "stories." Be sure the Search only in Elementary Schools button is selected.
5. Choose one of the school sites listed. Since links are often added, be sure to check this site in advance so you will be knowledgeable about what stories will be available to your students. This will guarantee success when you teach this lesson.

## Pre-Internet Activity:
Ask for several students to each volunteer to select and read their favorite journal story to the class. Review the process of a narration, if needed, before beginning. Then explain that they will have a chance to read what some other students across the country and Canada have written.

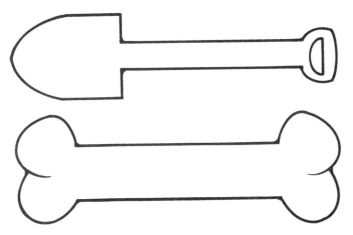

# ORIGINAL STORIES (cont.)

## Teaching the Lesson:

1. After sharing stories written by their classmates, students go online to read some stories written by other students. Follow the directions on page 58 to locate appropriate Web pages.

2. When visiting a school, mark its location on a map of the United States and Canada. You may have time to visit several sites listed by *Yahooligans!* Students may also wish to e-mail the creators of the stories to compliment them on their creativity or share how much they enjoyed their stories. (See "Electronic Mail" from pages 48 to 50.)

3. Lead a discussion about what the students liked or disliked about the authors' creations. Have them compare the stories they read on the Internet to those they read in class. Were there any similarities or differences? Which did they enjoy reading more? List with the students' help on the blackboard the qualities found in the stories which demonstrate good writing techniques.

4. Have the students continue working on the stories they read in class. Their trip to the Internet should have motivated them to produce their very best writing. If possible, publish the students' stories on the Internet on your school's home page. (See permission slip on page 98.)

## Extended Activities:

1. Students may also use the Internet to research topics about which they wish to write. Help them locate the Yahooligans! home page at http://www.yahooligans.com to further search for a topic of interest.

2. For more formal stories, try sharing some tales from the sites listed on page 115.

# REFERENCES

Dictionaries

Picture Dictionaries

Encyclopedias

Thesauruses

Other Internet Reference Resources

# DICTIONARIES

## Description
A world of words awaits students on the Internet at these dictionary sites.

## Objective(s):
- Alphabetize words.
- Search for definitions in an online dictionary.
- Identify parts of speech.
- Use new words from the dictionary in a story.

## Materials Needed:
- 6 copies of the bone pattern on page 62
- pail and sand shovel
- brown construction paper
- 1 copy of page 63 for each student

## Dictionary Web Sites:
**WWWebster Dictionary**
http://www.m-w.com/netdict.htm

**The Webster Dictionary**
http://elza.lpi.ac.ru/cgi-bin/wb

**The Oxford Concise Dictionary**
http://elza.lpi.ac.ru/cgi-bin/od

**OneLook Dictionary**
http://www.onelook.com/

## Pre-Internet Activity:
Write the words below on a cutout pattern of the bone from page 62. "Bury" them in a pail under crumpled brown construction paper. Ask for student volunteers to "dig up" a word, using a plastic sand shovel. Read the word to the class, and then have them guess as to the meaning of the word and whether it functions as a noun, verb, or adjective. Discuss where the students would go to find this information. Explain that they will be "digging up" the meanings of these words and their parts of speech in an online electronic dictionary.

| | |
|---|---|
| centaur | null |
| forage | pinnace |
| huckster | surrey |

# DICTIONARIES *(cont.)*

## Teaching the Lesson:

1. Distribute a copy of page 63 to each student. If desired, have the students first alphabetize the list of words from the pre-Internet activity on their papers by numbering them in the order in which they will occur.

2. Go online to one of the dictionary sites listed on page 61. Have the students follow the appropriate links to find the parts of speech and definitions of the words.

3. Challenge the students to write a short story using three of the new words they learned from the dictionary.

## Extended Activities:

1. Assign a pair of students to investigate the part of speech and meaning of a new word each week. Either provide a word for the students to reference, or allow them the freedom (under adult supervision) to find a new word on their own. Each new word is written on a bone pattern. The students write the part of speech on the shovel and definition on the handle of the shovel from the pattern below. Post the students' "word for the week" on a bulletin board entitled, "Digging Through the Dictionary."

2. While they are online, invite the students to search through a standard dictionary for the same words. How do the two resources compare? Which do they prefer to use? Why?

Name _____

# DIGGING THROUGH THE ONLINE DICTIONARY

**Directions:** Use an online dictionary to find the parts of speech and definitions of these words.

Example:

    nosh ( v. ) to eat a snack

1. huckster _____

_____

2. null _____

_____

3. pinnace _____

_____

4. forage _____

_____

5. centaur _____

_____

# PICTURE DICTIONARIES

## Description:
These sites will provide a motivating first dictionary experience for young learners.

## Objective(s):
- Identify beginning word sounds.
- Locate words in an online dictionary.
- Alphabetize words.

## Picture Dictionary Web Sites:
**Emmi's Critter ABCs**
http://web.aimnet.com/~veeceet/kids/abc_pg1.html

**Little Explorers**
http://www.enchantedlearning.com/Dictionary.html

## Ideas to Try Online:
1. For each letter study, visit one of the above sites to read words with each beginning sound. Students may also try to find words with specific ending sounds.

2. Have the students search for short or long vowel sounds that you may be studying. They can also try to find rhyming words for each long or short vowel sound.

3. Use the online picture dictionary to help students practice reading vocabulary words from their reading books. Which words can they find online?

4. Introduce ABC order. Have the students copy and illustrate on note cards five words with five different beginning letters from an online dictionary. They practice putting the cards in alphabetical order with a friend.

5. Each week choose three to five words for students to practice writing in sentences or in their creative stories.

6. Have one student select a "mystery word." The students ask yes and no questions to try to find the word in the online dictionary.

# ENCYCLOPEDIAS

## Description:
The encyclopedia is filled with interesting facts and information, and it's all just a click away when using an online encyclopedia resource.

## Objective(s):
- Understand the usefulness of an encyclopedia.
- Locate topics and information in the online encyclopedia.

## Materials Needed:
- 1 copy of page 67 for each student
- 1 copy of pages 68 and 69 for each pair of students

## Focus Web Site:

**Encyclopedia.com**
http://www.encyclopedia.com/home.html

About this site: Here you'll find a free, complete online encyclopedia reference which is as easy to use as clicking a mouse. Enter key words or use the volume reference to discover information on a variety of topics.

## Alternative Web Sites :*

**Knowledge Adventure Reference Station**
http://www.knowledgeadventure.com/encyclopedia

**Encyberpedia**
http://www.encyberpedia.com/ency.htm

## Pre-Internet Activity:
Give students the pop quiz on page 67. They should answer as best they can, guessing when necessary. Chances are the class will feel somewhat panicked since they probably do not know many (if any!) of the answers. Discuss which reference book would be most useful when finding the correct answers. Explain that they will have a chance to use an online encyclopedia to locate the correct answers and fix their quiz questions.

\* ***Author's note:*** *For serious online encyclopedia referencing, consider subscribing to Britannica Online at http://www.eb.com*

# ENCYCLOPEDIAS (cont.)

## Teaching the Lesson:

1. Discuss how an encyclopedia is different from other reference books, such as the dictionary or thesaurus.

2. Go online to the focus Web site. Enter the words from the answer column to read about each item. Then students browse the list of descriptors on page 67 for the correct one and change their answers.

3. Provide a copy of the card patterns from pages 68 and 69 for each pair of students.

   Illustrate each descriptor card.

   Illustrate each topic card by copying the picture drawn on the coordinating descriptor card.

## Extended Activities:

1. Invite individual students working under adult supervision to browse the volume listings for one other interesting topic. They write their topic and a brief summary on a note card and share what they learned with the class. Collect and use all the cards to play "Name That Fact" during free time. (**Instructions:** The teacher randomly chooses a topic from the pile of cards and asks students if they can summarize the topic.)

2. Do your students have a thirst for knowledge that just doesn't seem to be quenched? Visit the following site to learn fascinating facts and information that are sure to keep students talking for days! Pairs of students may visit here to gather the "fact for the week" to share with the class. Use this as a topic for students to further research (using traditional means) at a center.

   **Encyclopedia Smithsonian: FAQ**
   http://www.si.edu/resource/faq/start.htm

3. Before assigning that next research project, invite the class to go online with you to see what they can discover via the Internet first. After reading and compiling a beginning list of important facts, allow students to use more traditional means to further research their topics.

Name _____

# ENCYCLOPEDIA POP QUIZ!

Directions: Write the letter of the answer to each question on the lines. Then go online to the following Web site. Type in each topic, read the information, and then make changes as necessary.

**Encyclopedia.com** http://www.encyclopedia.com/home.html

1. _____ marsh land found in south Florida; a national park

2. _____ the process of green plants turning water and carbon dioxide into carbohydrates

3. _____ the capital of France

4. _____ the first person to create animated cartoons

5. _____ the science of living things

6. _____ the capital of Italy

7. _____ western settlers followed this 2,000 miles-long route

8. _____ the study of plant life

9. _____ a structure standing in upper New York Bay; became a national monument in 1924

10. _____ stream of gases that carry about one million tons of gas per second away from the sun

11. _____ invented scuba with Emil Gagnan

12. _____ a 10-foot Monitor that lives in Indonesia

A. Walter Elias Disney

B. Oregon Trail

C. Statue of Liberty

D. Everglades

E. Paris

F. Jacques Yves Cousteau

G. Komodo Dragon

H. Biology

I. Rome

J. Photosynthesis

K. Botany

L. Solar Wind

Name _____

# ENCYCLOPEDIA CONCENTRATION

**Directions:** Illustrate each topic below. Draw the same picture on its matching descriptor on page 69. Cut out the cards on the solid lines. Play "Encyclopedia Concentration" with a partner.

| | | |
|---|---|---|
| Walter Elias Disney | Oregon Trail | Statue of Liberty |
| Everglades | Paris | Jacques Yves Cousteau |
| Komodo dragon | biology | Rome |
| photosynthesis | botany | solar wind |

Name _____

# ENCYCLOPEDIA CONCENTRATION *(cont.)*

Use with page 68 to play "Encyclopedia Concentration."

| | | |
|---|---|---|
| Marshy land found in south Florida. It is also a national park. | The process when green plants turn water and carbon dioxide into carbohydrates. | The capital of France. |
| This person was one of the first to create animated cartoons. | The science of living things. | The capital of Italy. |
| Western settlers followed this route. It was 2,000 miles long! | The study of plant life. | This structure stands in New York Bay. It became a national monument in 1924. |
| Stream of gases that carries about 1 million tons of gas per second from the sun. | This person invented scuba with Emil Gagnan. | A 10-foot Monitor that lives in Indonesia. |

# THESAURUSES

## Description:

Tired of all those boring, repetitive words the students use in their writing? This online thesaurus activity will put an end to the doldrums and motivate students to write with a flourish.

## Objective(s):

- Brainstorm alternatives to everyday words.
- Search the online thesaurus for new words.

## Materials Needed:

- chart paper
- 1 copy of page 72 for each student
- sentence strips

## Thesaurus Reference Web Sites:

**Roget's Thesaurus**
http://www.thesaurus.com/
**or**
http://web.cs.city.ac.uk/text/roget/thesaurus.html

**WordNet**
http://www.cogsci.princeton.edu/~wn/

## Pre-Internet Activity:

Discuss a time when the students or someone they know was looking for "just the right word" to place in their writing but couldn't find what they were looking for. Explain that when looking for synonyms of words, people turn to a thesaurus. This is a reference book similar to a dictionary, but it usually lists just the parts of speech, synonyms, and antonyms of the entry words. Tell the class that they will have a chance to use an online thesaurus to find listings of synonyms for some words they know.

# THESAURUSES *(cont.)*

## Teaching the Lesson:

1. Display the following words on a chart. Have the students brainstorm additional words that mean the same or nearly the same thing. List the students' responses next to the vocabulary. Discuss reasons to select one word over another when writing.

       reward        sweet        rough        sneaky        few

2. Distribute a copy of page 72 to each student. Go online whcre students can search for the vase words in the thesaurus.Next they will cut out, match, and paste the vases with the correct flowers. Students will fill in the blank flower with an appropriate synonym.

3. Using page 72, the students work with a partner to think of a sentence for each entry word. They write their sentences on sentence strips, inserting blank lines instead of the words on the vases. The pairs read their sentences to the class. The class first figures out which word group belongs in the sentence and then decides on the best word from the list of six to enter into the sentences.

## Extended Activities:

1. Use thesaurus reference skills to "bury" some old, overused, meaningless words and instead provide students with lists of vivacious, interesting vocabulary to use in their places. Enlarge several patterns of the tombstone below. On each, write a word you notice the class overuses in their writing. (A sample list follows.) Assign each small group of students a word to reference. They write alternatives in the petals of the enlarged flower pattern below. Display the more appropriate words on the flowers over the graves of the "dead" words.

**"Dead" Words**
- bad
- good
- nice
- funny
- big
- happy
- like
- love
- neat
- cool
- stupid
- ugly

Name _____

# A THESAURUS BOUQUET

**Directions:** Each "bunch" of words also means the same as one of the words on the vases below. Enter the word on each of the vases into an online thesaurus reference to search for the correct group of words from the listing of alternative words. Choose one to write on the blank flower it belongs to. Cut and paste the vases under the correct bouquets of flowers.

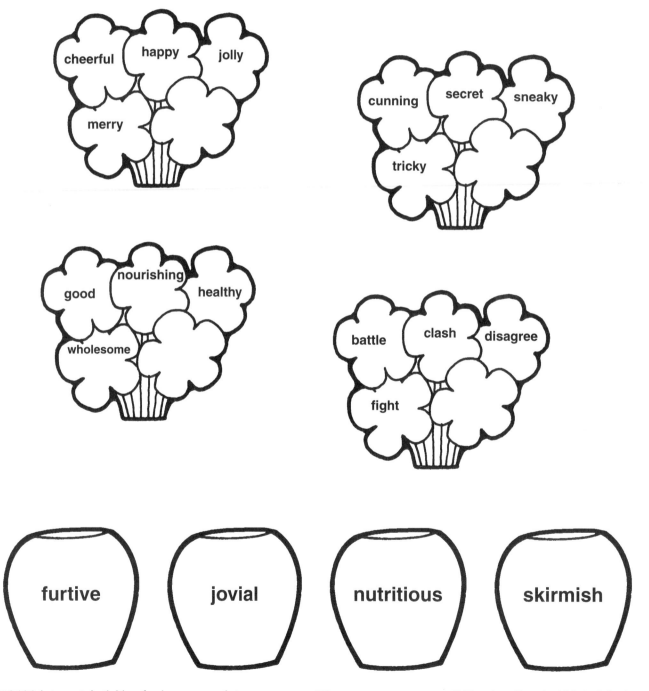

# OTHER INTERNET REFERENCE RESOURCES

The following miscellaneous sites provide a world of reference opportunities for students and teachers. Don't miss out on the unique learning experiences each has to offer!

## "Say What?"

**Quote Search**

http://www.starlingtech.com/quotes/

**Bartlett's Familiar Quotations**

http://www.columbia.edu/acis/bartleby/bartlett/

If you've ever wondered what famous (or not-so-famous) saying someone spoke regarding particular ideas, these sites will fill you in. Simply enter a key word, select a database, and then search to retrieve a host of familiar sayings regarding the word you entered. An excellent resource to improve creative and critical thinking skills. And remember... "The man who doesn't read good books has no advantage over the man who can't read them."—Mark Twain (key word, *book*)

## What's in a Word?

**Sniglets**

http://www.ithaca.edu/shp/shp99/rknight1/humor/sniglets.txt

Here you'll find a lengthy text document filled with valuable words you just can't find in the dictionary. Organized in dictionary style, students can learn a host of new words such as banectomy and vegeludes. Use this valuable reference to improve sentence writing, ABC order, creative writing, and decoding skills. (By the way, /snig' lit/, n. is any word that doesn't appear in the dictionary, but should. You'll have to look up *banectomy* and *vegeludes* for yourself!)

## Never at a Loss, for the Rhyming Word Boss

**Online Rhyming Dictionary**

http://www.link.cs.cmu.edu/dougb/rhyme-doc.html

If this site can't find the right rhyming word, it just can't be found! Use this reference to find rhymes for any word. Included, also, are homophone and synonym references and more.

# OTHER INTERNET REFERENCE RESOURCES *(cont.)*

## Y'all Come Back Now, Y'Hear?

**The Dictionary of American Regional English**
http://polyglot.lss.wisc.edu/dare/dare.html

During a study of the United States, be sure to reference this site to match the meanings of words and phrases to various regions of the U.S.

## My Special Day

**Famous Birthdays**
http://www.famousbirthdays.com/

Make students' birthdays extra-special by finding out which famous people share their special days. Visit this site whenever a student from class celebrates a birthday. Or go there just for fun! Select a particular month and day of the year or choose from one of several category links. There's even an online birthday quiz!

## It's All in the Past

**This Day in History**
http://www.historychannel.com/today/

Here's a place for students to reference notable events in history. This thought provoking site sponsored by the History Channel offers students a chance to take a step back in time to witness past events that occurred on today's date. Have pairs of students access this site daily or weekly to provide news reporting experience for students. Or post the information on a news-related bulletin board and provide comprehension or sequencing questions for use during center time.

# POETRY

Nursery Rhymes

Verse Poems

Shape Poems

Haiku

Thematic Poetry

Additional Poetry Ideas: Jungle Animals

Publishing Students' Poems

on the World Wide Web

# NURSERY RHYMES

## Description:
Mother Goose probably never expected to be flying on the Internet! These wholesome nursery rhymes are time honored classics that just happen to be available for viewing in cyberspace!

## Objective(s):
- Read and retell favorite rhymes.
- Apply rhyming skills.

## Materials Needed:
- chart paper
- 1 copy of page 78 for each student
- 1 white envelope for each student
- drawing paper

## Focus Web Site:
**Mother Goose Pages**
http://www-personal.umich.edu/~pfa/

**About this site:** This all-inclusive nursery rhyme site is sure to motivate both young and old to read on the Internet! Select one of the category links to search by main resources or theme. The theme link allows students to view titles by topics that interest them. Choose a poem, and then check the **History** link to read how the poem came to be. Other links include **Performance Tips**, a valuable resource for teachers, as well as **Music** and **Sources** links. Check them all out!

## Alternative Web Sites:
**Nursery Rhymes**
http:www-sqi.cit.gu.edu.au/~tracy/rhymes/

**Nursery Rhymes Collection**
http://www.geocities.com/EnchantedForest/Dell/3942/

**Zelo Nursery Rhymes**
http://www.zelo.com/family/nursery/index.html

# NURSERY RHYMES *(cont.)*

## Pre-Internet Activity:

Post one of your personal favorite nursery rhymes from the focus Web site on a chart, omitting the final rhyming words. Write the omitted words on note cards. Read the poem with the students. They place the rhyming words in the correct location on the chart. Explain to the students that they will have a chance to read and learn about more nursery rhymes on the Internet.

## Teaching the Lesson:

1. Use the focus Web site to check the students' answers from the pre-Internet activity.

2. Have the students orally share their favorite nursery rhymes with the class. Classmates should listen for the rhyming words in the poems. Write the words on the board or on cards as the students say their rhymes. Use them to practice matching rhyming words during future lessons about this topic.

3. Distribute a copy of page 78 to each student. Pre-read the nursery rhymes on the page, and have the students guess the rhyming words that might fit on the ends of the lines. Use the focus Web site to verify the students' answers. Then they write the answers on the lines.

4. Allow the class to decide where to go next. Ask for class volunteers to select themes and nursery rhymes to read off the Internet. After a suitable amount of time, give each student a sheet of drawing paper. Instruct the students to each illustrate their favorite nursery rhyme by using crayons or paints. Then they use scissors to cut the rhyme into four or five puzzle pieces. Give each student an envelope in which to keep his puzzle pieces. They each take their puzzle home and recite their favorite nursery rhyme to a parent or older sibling after putting the puzzle together.

## Extended Activities:

1. Get students in motion by inviting them to act out nursery rhymes. Print several of the nursery rhymes from the focus Web site while you are online with the class. Copy the poems onto charts so the whole class can join in. Select a poem, and read through it with the class once. Then ask for volunteers to come up to act out the rhyme as the class says it aloud.

2. Keep the posters from the first extended activity for use as reading warmups.

3. Place the posters at a center with crayons and drawing paper or suitable puppets or puppet-making supplies.

Name _____

# DO YOU HAVE TIME FOR A NURSERY RHYME?

Find this Web site: http://pubweb.acns.nwu.edu/~pfa/dreamhouse/ nursery/rhymes.html

**Directions:** Read the nursery rhymes. Try to guess the end rhyming words. Read the nursery rhymes at the Web site to see if you are correct. Write the rhymes in the lines.

**Theme:** Animals and other beasts     **Title:** I Had a Little Nut Tree

I had a little nut tree, nothing would it bear.

But a silver nutmeg and a golden _____.

The King of Spain's daughter came to visit me,

And all for the sake of my little nut _____.

I skipped over water, I danced over sea

And all the birds in the air couldn't catch _____.

**Theme:** Animals and other beasts     **Title:** Three Young Rats

Three young rats with black felt _____,

Three young ducks with white straw flats,

Three young dogs with curling _____,

Three young cats with demi-veils,

Went out to walk with two young _____

In satin vests and sorrel wigs,

But suddenly it chanced to _____

And so they all went home again.

---

## Word Bank

|       |      |      |      |
|-------|------|------|------|
| hats  | pigs | tree | pear |
| tails | rain | me   |      |

---

# VERSE POEMS

## Description:

A poem a day,
Keeps the teacher away!
So come spend some time,
As your class tries to rhyme!

## Objective(s):

- Write a poem.

## Materials Needed:

- 9 x 12 inch (23 cm x 30 cm) sheets of colorful construction paper

- 1 copy of page 82 for each student or pair of students (optional)

## Focus Web Site:

**KidzPage**
http://web.aimnet.com/~veeceet/kids/kidzpage.html

**About this site:** If prime examples of excellent poetry are what you seek, launch this Web site to fulfill your every wish! Select from one of several links, including verse poems by famous authors, an ABC verse poem, and student poetry published on the Web.

## Alternative Web Sites:

**Ken Nesbitt's Poetry for Children**
http://www.nesbitt.com/poetry/

**Grandpa Tucker's Rhymes and Tales**
http://www.night.net/tucker/

**Positively Poetry**
http://advicom.net/~e-media/kv/poetry1.html

## Pre-Internet Activity:

Ask the students to define the word poetry. In their definitions, did any of the students mention the word rhyme? Ask the class whether they enjoyed listening to nursery rhymes when they were younger. What was fun about them? Did they make sense? Have they ever wondered where those poems came from? To help get the students' rhyming brain waves in motion, visit one of the nursery rhyme sites listed on page 76. Explain that most of these poems fall under the category of verse poems since each line of the poem follows a certain beat or meter. (Please note that some poems are limericks or follow less specific rules.) Explain to the students that they should listen for the rhyming words so that they can share some later and tell where they are located in the poems.

# VERSE POEMS *(cont.)*

## Teaching the Lesson:

1. Now that your students are speaking in rhymes, have them put their creative rhyming talents to work writing verse poems. Have the students work in pairs to list as many rhyming words as they can on 9 x 12 inch (23cm x 30cm) sheets of colorful construction paper. All the words on each sheet must rhyme, but they may or may not follow the same spelling pattern (e.g., flute, suit, root, etc.) Some pairs of students may need as many as five or six sheets, depending on their rhyming skills. If necessary, provide a starting word at the top of each sheet. Use the list on the following page, if needed.

2. Post the rhyming posters on the chalkboard for everyone to see. Review the lists. As a class, determine whether all the words on each sheet belong on that page. Cross off any non-rhyming words and include any additional rhymes the students may think of as a class.

3. Visit the focus Web site as a class. Select one of the verse poem links: **Have a Bash with Ogden Nash, For Better or Verse, Verse and Worse!** If time allows, back up to the home page and try to link to all the poem pages. Invite the students to comment on any or all of the poems. Which were their favorites? Why? Tell them that they will now have a chance to use their rhyming lists to create a simple verse poem.

4. If desired, have the students work with partners. Demonstrate how to compose a verse poem for the class. First think of a person, place, or thing to write about. Then brainstorm ideas related to that object. Finally, work the thoughts and ideas into a simple two- or four-line rhyming poem. Students may use the poem planning sheet on page 82 to help get them started.

   Example:
   hippopotamus; fat, grey, teeth, water, tough skin, eats a lot

   > The hippopotamus is really fat,
   > He eats a lot, and that is that.
   > He'd never fit through any door,
   > Give him food—more, more, more!

5. Have the students rewrite their poems on blank or lined paper and then illustrate or decorate them. Publish the students' verses in a poem book or post them in the hallway for others to enjoy.

# VERSE POEMS *(cont.)*

## Sample Words to Rhyme

short a: cat, man, lad, pack, cap      long a: cape, save, lane, cake, ate, vase, mail

short e: let, men, sent, get, end      long e: green, bee, seal, feet, weed, dear

short i: pig, sip, fill, kiss, kid      long i: nine, five, bite, dime, smile

short o: top, fox, pot, dog, sock      long o: mole, cone, rope, rose, home

short u: sun, cub, chunk, mug, hut      long u: tube, mule, glue, suit, tune

## Extended Activities:

1. All the poems at the focus Web site are text only. Invite students to visit the Web site in pairs (with an adult chaperone) to find a poem that suits their fancy. They print the poem and the author and then either copy it in their best handwriting onto writing paper or cut and paste the verse onto drawing paper. Then they illustrate the poem to reflect their interpretation of the author's meaning.

2. A variation of the above is to select a favorite verse of your own, copy and post it (with the author's name) where all can see and then have all the students illustrate the same poem. After everyone is finished with his or her drawing, sit the class in a circle and have them share their pictures. Discuss any similarities or differences they notice among the illustrations and discuss how one reader's interpretation of a poem can be very different from someone else's. And that's what makes poetry so personal!

3. If students are having trouble thinking of rhyming words, be sure to introduce them to the online rhyming dictionary (see p. 73).

Name _____

# A VERSE POEM THAT WILL SURELY SHOW 'EM

A verse poem is a simple poem that usually rhymes at the end.

First think of some people, places, and things to write about. Remember, the more crazy the idea, the better!

| **People** | **Places** | **Things** |
|---|---|---|
| _____ | _____ | _____ |
| _____ | _____ | _____ |
| _____ | _____ | _____ |
| _____ | _____ | _____ |
| _____ | _____ | _____ |

From the above lists, circle the one thing that interests you the most. Write it in the circle. Now think of words that tell about that person, place, or thing. Write them around the outside of the circle.

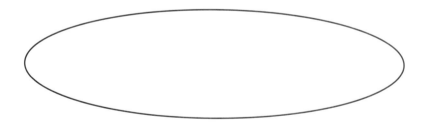

Use simple rhyming words to help you write a two- or four-line rhyming verse poem. The rhyming words should go at the end of each line.

Line 1: _____

Line 2: _____

Line 3: _____

Line 4: _____

# SHAPE POEMS

## Description:
Visit a flighty butterfly Web site and then create colorful poetry.

## Objective(s):
- Design a butterfly.
- Develop a word list which describes butterfly activities.
- Create a poem in a butterfly shape.

## Materials Needed:
- 1 copy of the butterfly pattern on page 86 for each student
- 1 copy of page 85 for each student (optional)
- ½ sheet of plain white or pastel-colored typing paper for each student
- 1 6 x 9 inch (15cm x 23cm) sheet of colorful construction paper for each student

## Focus Web Site:
**The Butterfly Web Site Internet Resource**
http://mgfx.com/butterfly/resource/index.htm

About this site: Choose your topic to learn what interests you about butterflies. The **Images** link displays a listing of butterfly picture sites. Or choose **Articles & Information** from the left of the Web page to read all about these delicate winged creatures.

## Alternative Web Sites:
**Butterfly Arc**
http://www.bassilichi.it/lorenzi/butterfly/frame.htm

**The South Carolina Butterfly Project**
http://butterfly.clemson.edu/

## Pre-Internet Activity:
Supply the students with a copy of the butterfly outline on page 86. Instruct them to color and decorate the butterfly with their crayons. If possible, go on a mini butterfly hunt to observe butterflies in their natural setting. If an outdoor sojourn just isn't possible, students should bring their butterfly drawings outside and try to imagine how they would look if they were real. Allow students to share their creations. Have the class list on the board any thoughts, feelings, or descriptions that come to mind when they look at the pictures and think about how butterflies act in the wild. Explain that the students will visit an Internet site that will tell all about butterflies.

# SHAPE POEMS *(cont.)*

## Teaching the Lesson:

1. Launch the focus Web site with the class. From the left of the screen, click on the **Articles & Information** link to select a topic of interest to read about butterflies. Instruct the students to be thinking of additional ideas they could add to the list begun during the pre-Internet activity.

2. If time allows, go to the **Butterfly Gallery** link to view pictures of butterflies. Have the students tell how the butterflies on the Internet are alike or different from the pictures they have colored.

3. Return to the list on the board. Have the students add any additional thoughts or ideas that came to mind while on the Internet.

4. Have the students complete additional research to complete the information sheet on page 85. They may use this to further develop their list of butterfly ideas.

5. Distribute half of a plain sheet of typing paper to each student. Demonstrate how to place the blank sheet over the decorated butterfly from the pre-Internet activity and tape in place. Then show the students how to write words associated with butterflies on the outline they see through the blank sheet (like tracing, only with words instead of lines).

6. Students mount their poems on a colorful sheet of 6 x 9 inch (15cm x 23cm) construction paper. Then they cut out the colored butterfly. Use the cutouts as a border around a bulletin board. Display the students shape poems within the butterfly border.

## Extended Activity:

Allow students to investigate sites about ice cream, teddy bears, and planet Earth to complete additional shape poems centered around these topics. (shapes on pages 86 and 87)

**Ice Cream**
http://www.foodsci.uoguelph.ca/
dairyedu/icecream.html

**Earth Introduction**
http://heasarc.gsfc.nasa.gov/docs/StarChild/ (click on **Solar System** and then **Earth**)

**Theodore and Tilly-Bear's Fun Site**
http://members.aol.com/lmicklus/tbears/index.htm
(select the **Things to Read** link)

Name _____

# BUTTERFLY BONANZA!

**Find this Web site:** The Butterfly Web Site Internet Resource

**Directions:** Use what you learned on the Internet and other resources to complete this information page about butterflies. Write additional words to describe butterflies on the back of this page. Use your lists to make a shape poem about butterflies.

**Where Butterflies Live**

**Different Kinds of Butterflies**

**What Butterflies Look Like**

**What Butterflies Eat**

**How Butterflies Act**

**Other Information About Butterflies**

# BUTTERFLY BONANZA! *(cont.)*

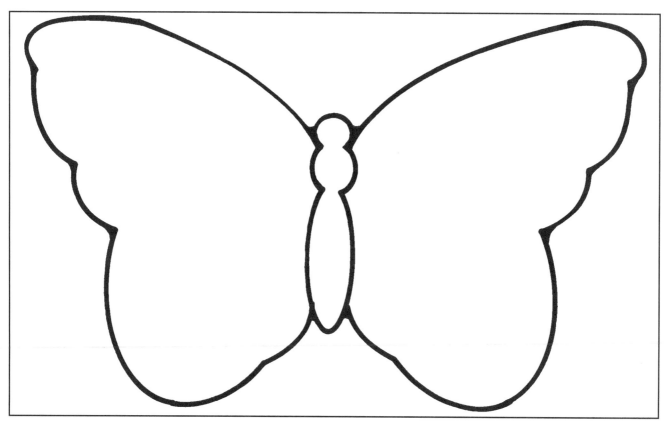

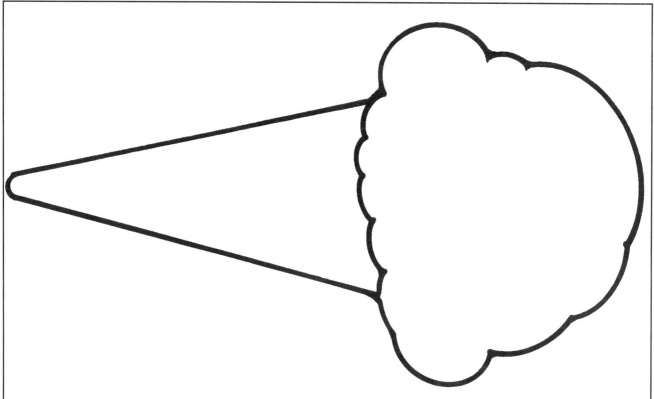

# BUTTERFLY BONANZA! *(cont.)*

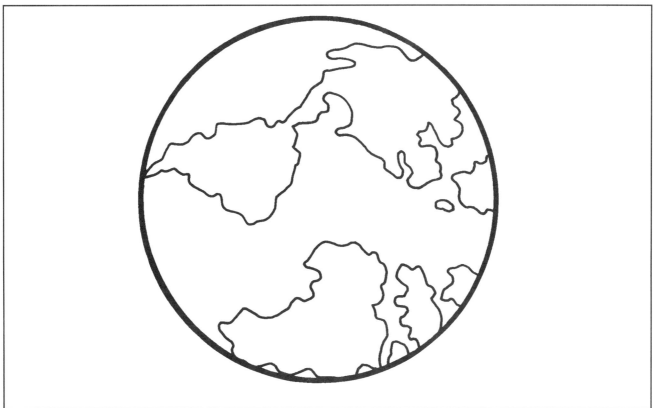

# HAIKU

## Description:

Students will be in tune with nature when they carefully and quietly observe the elements of creation with their senses. Discoveries will be used to write haiku poems.

## Objective(s):

- Observe nature on an outdoor walk.
- Write observations on paper.
- Read examples of Haiku.
- Compose a Haiku poem.

## Materials Needed:

- two or three blindfolds
- 1 copy of page 90 for each student (optional)
- 1 sheet of parchment paper for each student
- black ink markers

## Focus Web Site:

**The Haiku Habit**
http://members.aol.com/Jemrich/haikuhabit.index.html

**About this site:** From a simple definition to specific examples, students will learn the true value of haiku poetry and its potential usefulness as a poem for observing nature.

## Alternative Web Sites:

**Haiku**
http://www.faximum.com/aha.d/haiku.htm

**Logos & Haiku**
http://www.bekkoame.or.jp/~ryosuzu/index.html

**The Shiki Internet Haiku Salon**
http://mikan.cc.matsuyama-ac.jp/~shiki

## Pre-Internet Activity

To prepare for a nature walk in which the students make mental observations about their journey, instruct the students to use as many senses as they can: sight, smell, hearing, touching. Have the students find a quiet spot to simply sit and observe. Select two or three students to blindfold during the observation time. Reinforce the concept of quiet observation; the students should not talk to one another. After five to ten minutes, gather the class together again. Sit under a tree in the shade and allow the students to share their observations. Compare the lists of the seeing observers to the lists of those who were blindfolded. Were their experiences different? How?

# HAIKU *(cont.)*

## Teaching the Lesson:

1. Upon returning to class, have the students jot down some observations they found particularly meaningful: the soaring of a bird, the buzz of a bee, the rustle of leaves, etc. Then have them list related thoughts or ideas to accompany their observations:

    leaves rustling, crunching, green and gold, wind, dotted light

2. Explain to the students that a haiku poem is a special kind of Japanese poetry that relies on nature for its ideas. It also follows special syllable requirements.

3. If necessary, review syllables by using the student activity page (90).

4. Launch the focus Web site with the class. Read the author's description and simple guidelines to write haiku poetry and then read the examples listed on the page. Invite the students to comment on any or all of the author's poems.

5. Have the students review their observation lists to compose a haiku poem. Although the author suggests poems be three lines following only a short-long-short pattern between 10 to 14 syllables total, you may wish to instruct the students to attempt a more traditional poem by following the 5-7-5 syllable format.

    Leaves up in the trees

    Rustling, crunching, tumbling, soft

    Gold and green sunlight

6. After the students are satisfied with their poems, distribute a sheet of light-colored parchment paper and a black-ink marker to each student for them to use to copy their poems in their best handwriting in the center of the paper. Then they may use crayons, markers, or colored pencils to illustrate their poems. Display them in the hall for all to see on a bulletin board entitled, "Haiku in Nature." Or, if preferred, combine the poems into one book with the same title and place it in the library for others to enjoy.

## Extended Activity:

1. Students may enjoy a virtual tour of Japan to accompany their study of haiku poetry. A link to one of the following sites will provide students with valuable information about one of the world's most exotic countries.

**Kids Web Japan**
http://www.jinjapan.org/kidsweb/

**Kid's Window**
http://www.jwindow.net/KIDS/

Name _____

# SIMPLY SYLLABLES

A syllable is the part of a word with its own vowel sound.  Look at the words.  Say them out loud.  Clap your hands to show each syllable.

| Word | Syllables & Vowel Sounds | Word Divided into Syllables | |
|---|---|---|---|
| bunch | bunch | bunch | (1) |
| art | art | art | (1) |
| simply | sim - plee | sim - ply | (2) |
| happy | hap - pee | hap - py | (2) |
| syllable | sil - la - b l | syl - la - ble | (3) |
| government | gov - ern – ment | gov - ern - ment | (3) |

Look at each word.  Clap the syllables.  Write the number of syllables on the lines.

1. _____ children

2. _____ family

3. _____ stone

4. _____ clothesline

5. _____ news

6. _____ music

7. _____ page

8. _____ neighborhood

9. _____ information

10. _____ frog

11. _____ game

12. _____ museum

13. _____ birthday

14. _____ house

15. _____ kitchen

Now read the following phrases and sentences.  Clap the number of syllables you hear in each phrase or sentence.  Write the number on the lines.

16. _____ The fat cat sat.

17. _____ Jim ate a snake.

18. _____ Mister Jones went on a fishing trip.

19. _____ forgotten door

20. _____ funny clowns on parade

21. _____ information highway

# THEMATIC POETRY

## Description:

No matter what subject you are teaching, having students create a unique poem about a specific topic is an excellent way to discover their true comprehension of the subject matter.

## Objective(s):

- Locate information on a topic.

- Write a free-verse poem.

## Teaching the Lesson:

Spend fifteen to twenty minutes searching for a suitable Web site centered around the topic at hand. (The example that follows culminates a unit about frogs.) Access the site with the class to reinforce the topic. As they read, they should identify known information and discuss new information. Then allow the students to create a free verse poem (or other of your choosing) about that topic. The Internet connection really motivates students to apply their creative thinking skills!

## Example:

Topic:       Frogs*

Web site:    Frogland
             http://www.teleport.com/~dstroy/frogland.html

**Before beginning**: Give students a green construction paper frog pattern to trace and cut out. While at the Web site, students can list new information on their frog patterns.

**Poetry connection:** Students use their frog lists to create an informational acrostic poem about frogs.

no Fur

no wa Rts

gOod luck in Japan

polliwo Gs

amphibianS

\* See "Synonyms" from pages 38 to 40.

# ADDITIONAL POETRY IDEAS: JUNGLE ANIMALS

## Description:

Free expression without grammatical rules...what genre of writing could be more inviting for students? Delve into the more articulate side of poetry by providing on-the-Net activities centered around the topics found in the "Teaching the Lessons" section.

## Objective(s):

- Explore poetry on the Internet.
- Use creative thinking skills.

## Materials Needed:

- chart paper
- Margaret Mahy's book, *17 Kings and 42 Elephants*

## Pre-Internet Activity:

Discuss each of the following sound devices poets use to create acoustically pleasing and fun-to- read poems. List examples for the students on chart paper and then have them add to the lists by thinking of additional ideas as a class. Read Margaret Mahy's *17 Kings and 42 Elephants*. This book is filled with examples of each of the four devices that follow (and many more that aren't discussed in this guide). After reading, have the students cite examples from the poem and add them to the charts. Explain that the students will have a chance to explore each sound device themselves as they discover more about some of the animals from the story on the Internet.

## Teaching the Lessons:

### Onomatopoeia: Elephants

These are words that sound like their meanings: bang, crunch, pop, squeak, etc.

1. Have the students list any information they already know about elephants on a chart. Visit any of the Web sites about elephants listed on page 95. As they read, students add to their lists of elephant facts. Then they review the chart listing onomatopoeic words. Demonstrate how to write a simple four-line poem including at least one fact and three onomatopoeic words. Have the students write them on elephant-shaped cutouts and post them on a bulletin board entitled "Toot! Toot! From the Elephant's Snoot."

> The elephant's tusks are big and white,
> They **crunch** a tree in just one bite.
> His feet **boom** on the forest floor,
> But he can't **squeak** through the kitchen door!

# ADDITIONAL POETRY IDEAS: JUNGLE ANIMALS *(cont.)*

## Teaching the Lessons *(cont.)*

### Assonance: Tigers

These are words that have the same vowel sounds. They may or may not rhyme: glad, clap, ramble, can, etc.

1. Divide the class into ten groups, one for each long and short vowel sound. Assign a long or short vowel sound to each group. They spend ten minutes thinking of words that have their vowel sound. Explain that the words do not have to rhyme. After their brainstorming session, invite students to join you on the computer as you browse the Web sites (p. 95) about tigers. The students should pay attention to the information they read so they can use it in the group poem they will write about tigers.

2. After visiting the Web site, the students work with their groups to write a simple free-verse poem using the information they learned as well as at least five words from their long or short vowel list. Have the students copy the poems in black ink in their best handwriting on plain paper and then lightly color it with orange and black stripes to resemble tiger stripes. They may also wish to include some eyes peering out from the top to give the illusion of the tiger eyeing its reader. Post the students' work in the hallway in a jungle-like setting, if possible.

> His coat hides his own,
> He is more bold on the road,
> And his nose sniffs prey in the cold.

### Consonance: Primates

These words have repeated consonant sounds anywhere within the words: chair, catcher, patch.

1. As a class, decide on a sound everyone will focus on. Visit one of the Web sites about primates (monkeys) listed on page 95. Have the students work with partners. As the class visits the Web site, the partners should list as many words as they can find with that sound. Remind students that the sound may appear in the beginning, middle, or end of the word. Challenge the class to be the group with the most words. Reward them with a free homework pass or other simple token.

2. Allow a few groups to share their lists so that students whose lists are brief may acquire a few more ideas. Have the students work with their partners to create unique poems about monkeys with a focus on consonant sounds. (See the example on the following page.) They write their final drafts on banana-shaped cutouts. Create a bulletin board display by attaching the bananas to a large tree with monkeys swinging from its branches.

# ADDITIONAL POETRY IDEAS: JUNGLE ANIMALS *(cont.)*

## Teaching the Lessons *(cont.)*
### Consonance: Primates *(cont.)*

> Ta**m**arins and **M**ar**m**osets,
> S**m**all **m**onkeys of the A**m**azon,
> **M**ischievous as the **m**yths of gre**m**lins,
> But ta**m**e for **m**en and wo**m**en.

### Alliteration: Exotic Birds
These words all have the same beginning consonant sounds: bubble, bank, bewilder, baron.

1. Visit one of the Web sites about exotic birds (parrots) listed on page 95. Tell the class they should be listening for information about the birds so that they can create a list of related words after they log off.

2. Divide the class into groups of two to four students each. Provide each group with a copy of the chart on page 96. Each group first decides on a beginning sound on which to focus. Then they work together to list under each category as many words as possible that start with the sound they identified at the top of the page.

3. Using their lists, students write an alliterative sentence about parrots or other exotic birds on a sentence strip. Allow time for the groups to share their alliterative sentences.

4. Then the students transfer their alliterative sentences onto feathers to create poems. Set out a variety of colorful construction paper. After choosing a color, each group cuts a featherout of the paper and writes the alliterative sentence on it. Display the students' colorful work with the heading "Perfect Plumage."

**Example:**

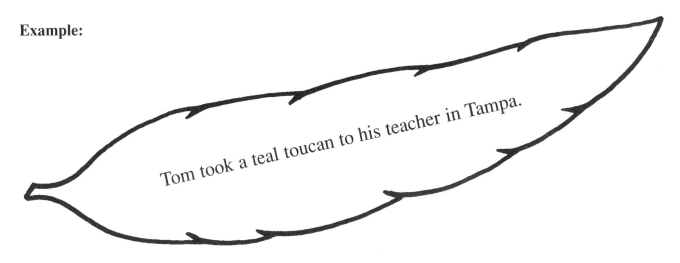

Tom took a teal toucan to his teacher in Tampa.

# ADDITIONAL POETRY IDEAS:

## Jungle Animals *(cont.)*

Use these Web sites to enrich Margaret Mahy's *17 Kings and 42 Elephants* and use in conjunction with the additional ideas described in the preceding pages. Or, select an animal of your choice, do a quick search on the Internet, and use the ideas with the animal of your choosing.

## Elephants

**Elephant**
http://pantheon.yale.edu/~ciampor/elephant.html

**ADDO Elephant National Park**
http://www.jan.ne.jp/~kawabe/addo/

**A Page of Information on Elephants**
http://www.inactive.demon.co.uk/elephant.html

## Tigers

**Tiger Information**
Center http://www.5tigers.org/

**Tigers!**
http://www.tiger.to/

**All for Tigers!**
http://www.tiger.to/

## Primates (Monkeys)

**The Primate Gallery**
http://www.selu.com/~bio/PrimateGallery/

**Tiny Monkeys**
http://www.pbs.org/wnet/nature/gremlins/html/intro.html

**Duke University Primate Center**
http://www.duke.edu/web/primate/home.html

## Exotic Birds (Parrots)

**The Dutch Parrot Refuge**
http://www.IAEhv.nl/users/nop/

**The Online Book of Parrots**
http://www.ub.tu-clausthal.de/p_welcome.html

**Parrot Pages**
http://users.netonecom.net/~schripdd/ParrotPages.html

# JUNGLE BIRDS ALLITERATION

Name _____

**Directions:** Decide on a beginning sound. Write it in the space provided. Use what you learned about exotic birds to list under each category as many words as you can think of that begin with the same sound. Use the words to write a sentence on the line below.

Beginning Sound

| people | places | things | ideas | verbs (action) | adjectives (describing) | adverbs (how) |
|--------|--------|--------|-------|----------------|-------------------------|---------------|
|        |        |        |       |                |                         |               |

Sensational Sentence:

# PUBLISHING STUDENTS' POEMS ON THE WORLD WIDE WEB

Most teachers would agree that an important step of any creative writing assignment is publishing students' work. Whether simply posting their creations on a bulletin board, creating a class book, having the students read them to another adult in the school, or submitting them to your local paper (to name but four publishing ideas), students need to know that what they produce has meaning and is worthy of publication and sharing. What better way is there to voice this sentiment than to publish your students' poems where anyone in the world may have access to them?

The following Web sites provide information on how to go about submitting student entries. Some require e-mail; others may be sent via "snail mail." You may be asked to complete a registration form. Some offer the opportunity to place a class picture or the individual student's picture with his or her work. Access any of the following sites and follow the links (if necessary) to read about what is expected of both you and your students to publish poems on the Web.

**Poetry Pals' K–12 Student Poetry Publishing Project**
http://www.geocities.com/EnchantedForest/5165/

**Kid Pub**
http://www.kidpub.org/kidpub/howto.html

**Positively Poetry**
http://advicom.net/~e-media/kv/poetry1.html

Regardless of the extent to which you wish to publish your students' poems on the World Wide Web, first ask whether the students are interested in viewing their poems on a Web site. Then notify parents of your intentions. (Use the permission slip on page 98.)

Last but not least, don't forget to set aside time to visit the Web site so the students see their work!

Dear Parents:

We are practicing our correspondence skills by e-mailing postcards to friends and relatives. If you know of someone who would enjoy receiving a message from your son or daughter, please fill out the information below and return this slip with your child. We will be e-mailing on (date) _____. Thank you for supporting our technology activities!

Sincerely,

_____

Our child, _____, may e-mail the following person:

_____ Friend?    Relative?

His or her e-mail address is

_____

Signed:

_____

---

Dear Parents:

We have been working very hard on our writing skills. And now we have the opportunity to share them with the whole world! This form gives your child permission to post his or her writing on the World Wide Web. Please note that we may also include a picture of your child (either a class picture or an individual picture) to accompany the writing. Students will be listed on a first-name-only basis. Please sign the form below to give permission for us to post our writing on the Web.

Sincerely,

_____

_____ Yes! I give permission for my child, _____ to post his/her writing on the World Wide Web.

May we include your child's picture?    Yes    No

_____ No, I do not wish my child's writing to be posted on the World Wide Web.

Child's name: _____

Signed: _____

# READING

Fables

Fairy Tales

Interactive Stories

Myths and Legends

Just for Fun: Stories on the Web

# FABLES

## Description:
Our days are filled with valuable lessons learned.  Here is a chance to share some in-depth lessons in the form of literature: fables.

## Objective(s):
- Read and interpret fables.
- Create a moral for a fable.
- Write a fable incorporating the moral.

## Materials Needed:
- pocket chart and sentence strips (optional)
- large lined note cards
- decorated shoebox

## Focus Web Site:
**Aesop's Fables Online**
http://www.pacificnet.net/~johnr/aesop/

About this site: Arranged in alphabetical order by title, these fables allow the viewer to read the moral in advance and then read the fable.  The morals and fables are a bit wordy, but with discussion about the events in the fable, students should be able to decipher the meanings of the fables in their own words.

## Alternative Web Sites:
**Aesop's Fables** (gopher site; text only)
http://attila.stevens-tech.edu/~soh1/aesop.html

**Fluency Through Fables**
http://www.comenius.com/fable/index.html

## Pre-Internet Activity:
Begin a discussion about what the students have learned in school.  What kinds of lessons do they learn in school that also apply at home, on the bus, or at play? Explain that a *moral* is a rule we follow to guide us to do the right thing.  Ask for a few volunteers to tell about a time when someone they knew didn't want to share.  What do they think that person should have done differently? What lesson do they hope that person learned? Next explain to the class that a story that teaches a simple moral like sharing is called a fable.  Aesop's fables are the most popular kind of fable, although other authors have also written fables.  Tell the students that they will have a chance to read some of Aesop's fables on the Internet and decide the moral of the stories.

# FABLES (cont.)

## Teaching the Lesson:

1. Post the following "lessons" on the chalkboard or in a pocket chart. Divide the class into groups of three students each to discuss the importance of each rule of behavior. Then each group decides on the most important lesson and group members recall when they or a friend learned a life lesson about that rule. Come together as a class, have each group share one anecdote concerning one lesson, and then tally the ones the class thinks are the most important rules to follow.

   | | |
   |---|---|
   | sharing | leaving things alone that don't belong to you |
   | making friends | including others |
   | respecting adults | doing things you're told to do |
   | listening | doing your best |
   | being kind to others | taking care of your things |

2. Explain that the fables the students are about to read are much like the stories they just told, only they usually involve animal characters. The students should listen to the fable to decide on a reasonable moral for the story.

3. Launch the focus Web site with the class. Select one of Aesop's links and then review the list of titles and morals. (You may want to visit the site ahead of time and pick out the fables that you wish to read with the class.) Click the fable link and read the story with the class. After each fable, discuss the events that took place and the lesson the character should have learned. What do they think he or she will do differently next time?

4. After reading 10 to 12 (or more!) fables and morals with the class, have students add any additional and important lessons to the list from step 1. Discuss how the students could change the stories they told from step 1 and/or the pre-Internet activity into fables by making the characters animals instead of people. Rewrite one of the student's stories together as a class. Include the moral at the end.

5. Provide each student with a large lined note card. They write and illustrate an original fable on one side of the card, and write the moral of the story (using the list from steps 1 and 4) on the opposite side. Place all the student-made fables in a decorated shoebox. Each day, to start the day, pull a story at random from the box. Read the student's fable to the class. The class shares what they think the moral of the story is. Flip the card over to divulge what the author said the moral of the story was.

6. After all the fables have been read, arrange all the cards so all the stories are facing up. Place a blank card on top of the stack and write the title, Mr. or Mrs. (your name)'s Fables. Invite one student to decorate the title card. Link all the cards with a ring and place them in the reading corner for the students to enjoy in their free time.

# FABLES *(cont.)*

## Extended Activities:

1. Fables are short, easily remembered stories the students will enjoy retelling. Invite pairs of students to visit the focus Web site, select a fable the class didn't read together, and then role-play the fable for the class or simply retell it during oral reading time. The class then discusses and decides on the moral of the story and confirms it with the two storytellers.

2. What good is learning one of life's many lessons if you're not going to apply it the next time you find yourself in a similar situation? List the fables' titles on a chart as you read them as a class (step 3 from "Teaching the Lesson"). Divide the class into groups, one for each title. Write each title at the top of a large note card. The students then illustrate and rewrite the fable, changing the events and the ending so that the character "does the right thing." After the students have completed their rewrites, they secure the card to a sheet of drawing paper and illustrate it. Then the groups share their new stories with the class. Post the students' work on a bulletin board entitled "Lessons Learned!"

# FAIRY TALES

## Description:
Students consider the characters and events that pit "good" against "evil" in several classic tales when they read stories on the Net.

## Objective(s):
- Share fairy tales.
- Classify events/characters as good or evil.
- Create a board game about a fairy tale.
- Understand that fairy tales have good endings.

## Materials Needed:
- chalkboard
- colorful construction paper
- 1 copy of pages 105 and 106 for each group of students
- letter-size file folder for each group of students
- small game tokens and one die for each group of students

## Focus Web Site:
**Grimm's Fairy Tales**
http://www.ul.cs.cmu.edu/books/GrimmFairy/

## Alternative Web Sites:
**Brothers' Grimm Fairy Tales**
http://www.lochnet.com/49845/rec/arts/books/childrens/grimm.htm

**Fairy Tales (Gopher Menu)**
gopher://ftp.std.com/11/obi/book/Fairy.Tales/Grimm

## Pre-Internet Activity:
List the titles of the following popular fairy tales on the board. Under each title, list the words "good" and "evil." Invite students, one at a time, to share a simple retelling of the story. The rest of the class should be listening for good and bad characters and events that take place in the tale. After each retelling, ask the students to list three characters and/or events under each heading. Write the students' responses on the board.

| Hansel & Gretel | | Cinderella | | Snow White | |
|---|---|---|---|---|---|
| Good | Evil | Good | Evil | Good | Evil |

Place the students into groups of three to four students each. Assign the groups the task of thinking of one additional fairy tale title and listing the good and evil aspects from the story. Students write their responses on large pieces of colorful construction paper. Allow time for the groups to share their ideas.

# FAIRY TALES *(cont.)*

## Teaching the Lesson:

1. For pleasant reading on the World Wide Web, share some lesser known fairy tales from the focus Web site. Students should again be listening for good and evil characters and events in the stories. Explain that many fairy tales follow this simple "good against evil" story line, but the endings almost always come out in favor of good conquering over evil.

2. Working again with their groups from the pre-Internet activity, have the students decide on a fairy tale they wish to make into a game. It may be one discussed during the pre-Internet activity, one from the Web, or one of their own choosing. Distribute a copy of the blank game boards on pages 105 and 106. Explain the directions to the students and then give them time to make their fairy tale games. They may cut out the completed board and glue it on the inside of a letter-sized file folder. Then they decorate the front of the folder with the title of the fairy tale and a colorful illustration.

3. Collect all the game boards and redistribute them to different groups to play with. Students may use any small token for a game piece (some more creative groups may have made game pieces for their boards). Each group will also need one number cube. Allow a reasonable amount of time for the groups to play and then recollect and redistribute the boards as time allows.

## Extended Activity:

1. Discuss the topic of characterization. Help the students decide which actions or events make the fairy tale characters "good" or "evil." Allow the students to work with a partner to create finger puppets of the main characters in a fairy tale. (The pattern to the right may aid students in this assignment.) Then they practice retelling the story to each other using their puppets to "speak" lines from the story. Allow a few minutes each day for the partners to share their retelling during reading time. (This idea also makes a great center activity.)

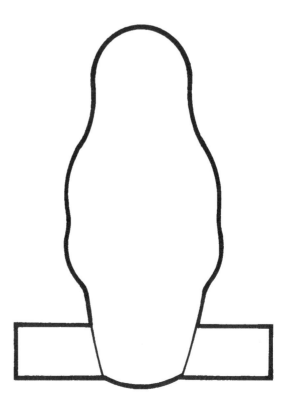

Name _____

# FAIRYLAND GAME BOARD

**Directions:** Think about your favorite fairy tale. List some good characters and events and evil characters and events in the story on a sheet of paper. Now use your list to create a game board of your fairy tale. Write about good events and have something good happen in the game. Write about evil events and have something bad happen in the game. Only write in the blanks that have dark lines. Color and decorate your game board. Glue it inside a file folder. Write and illustrate the title of the fairy tale on the cover of the folder.

**Example:**   **Good:** The creatures make Cinderella a dress. Go ahead three spaces.

  **Bad:** Cinderella's stepsisters treat her meanly. Lose one turn.

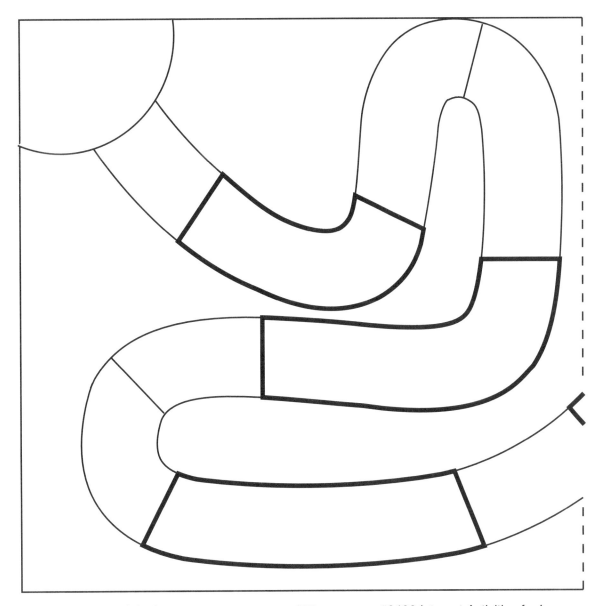

# FAIRYLAND GAME BOARD (cont.)

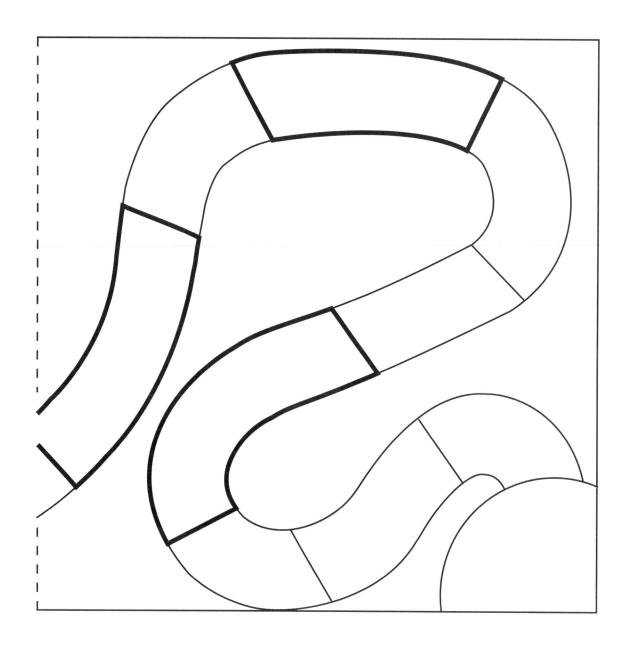

# INTERACTIVE STORIES

## Description:

What would have happened if Jack hadn't sold the cow for beans? Scrooge had changed his ways after the first ghostly visit? Students consider the importance of events in a story.

## Objective(s):

- Summarize events of a story.
- Practice sequencing skills.
- Create their own tale on the Web.

## Materials Needed

- 1 copy of the animals on page 110
- sentence strips
- 1 copy for each student of the octopus head from page 110.
- 2 x 18 inch (5 cm x 46 cm) strips of colorful construction paper

## Focus Web Site

**The Never Ending Tale**
http://www.coder.com/creations/tale/

**About this site:** This site offers a collection of stories where the readers decide the stories' endings. Simple instructions for young readers accompany the site. It also provides a little something for parents and teachers to read prior to engaging young learners.

## Alternative Web Sites

**Tales from the Internet: Mike Rofone, Roving Reporter**
http://www.indigo.ie/local/mikero/index.html

**Hillside's Choose Your Own Adventure**
http://hillside.coled.umn.edu/class1/Buzz/Story.html

**Planet Blortland**
http://www.bonus.com/bonus/card/infloatour.html

## Pre-Internet Activity

Copy and cut apart the animal pictures on page 110. Read the following short story. Explain to the students that they should be listening to the order in which the animals appear in the story.

Frog was looking for a friend to play with. He hopped along to gopher's house, but gopher was hiding in his hole. He tried owl's, but owl was sleeping in his tree. Next he went to robin's, but she was busy feeding her young. Then he tried alligator, but alligator threatened to eat him. He didn't want to play that way! Frog went home, afraid he would have to give up looking for someone to play with. He had almost reached his pad when toad called to him and asked him to play. The two new friends played all day.

# INTERACTIVE STORIES *(cont.)*

## Pre-Internet Activity *(cont)*

Distribute the animal cutouts to the students who think they were listening very well. Instruct them to come to the front of the room, one at a time, in the order in which they appeared in the story. After the line is formed, ask the class to check their order. Read the story once again to verify the students' positions. Ask the students if the order in which frog approached the animals was very important in the story. Ask them to tell about a time when following the correct order is very important *(following a recipe)* or not so important *(doing a list of chores)*. Explain that they will get to read some stories on the Internet where they get to decide the order of events. Each time they decide what will happen next, the story will be different than if they'd selected something else.

## Teaching the Lesson

1. Distribute a sentence strip to each pair of students. Log onto the focus Web site as a class and decide on a story to "create." Read the first page of the story and demonstrate how to summarize the events in one sentence on a sentence strip.

2. Allow each pair of students a turn at the computer. Each pair selects an option, reads the page they selected, and summarizes the events on their sentence strip. (Explain to the students that once a link is selected, they cannot go back and select a different one.)

   (Another option is to link through the story as a class but still allow pairs to summarize the events on each page. If the story ends and pairs are left without turns, allow them to go first the next day. Likewise, if the story is not ended and all the pairs have had a turn, finish the story as a class.)

3. Collect the sentence strips in order. After all the pairs have had a turn on the Internet, gather the students in a circle in the order in which they took turns on the Internet. Redistribute the sentence strips, and read the story the class "created." Assign an adult volunteer to type or word-process this story.

4. Follow this same procedure a second day with the same story to see how the story changes. Explain that students may not select a link that has already been chosen. (The links change color once selected.)

5. Have the class make a sequence octopus of one of the two interactive stories. Distribute a copy of the octopus head from page 110 and eight 2 x 18 inch (5 cm x 46 cm) construction paper strips of varied colors. They color and decorate the octopus' head and then copy eight sentences from the story onto the construction paper. (Students may need to omit some events.) Then they glue the sentence strips in order from left to right on the bottom of the octopus' head. (See the example on page 109.)

# INTERACTIVE STORIES *(cont.)*

## Extended Activities*

1. Writing different endings is a great way to get students to consider the events of a story and further their understanding. The next time you read a story as a class, have each student write a different ending. Allow time for the students to share their new finales and make positive comments regarding each other's creativity.

2. The next time you read a story orally, stop at the climax of the story and have pairs of students write an original ending. Allow time for the pairs to share and then read the author's conclusion. Take a class poll to see who guessed the author's intentions correctly. Which of all the endings (students and author alike) did the class like the best? Why? Discuss whether the students have ever read a book which they wished had ended differently. How would they have changed the ending? Why?

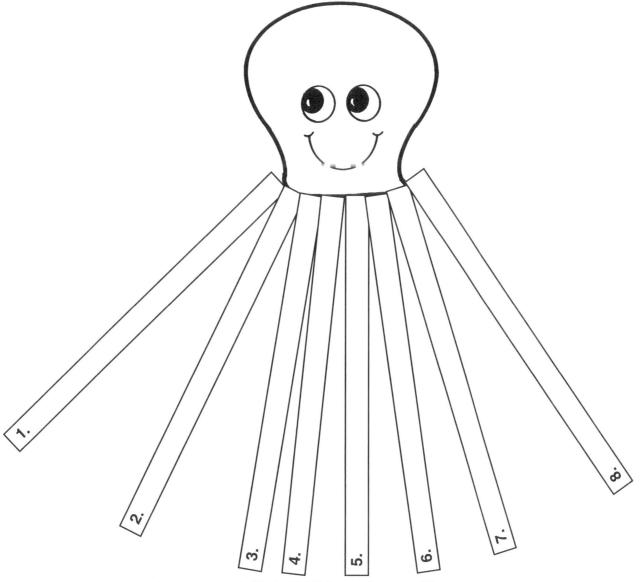

* *Author's Note: Be sure to also experience the Wacky Web Tales site (see page 33).*

# INTERACTIVE STORIES *(cont.)*

# MYTHS AND LEGENDS

## Description:
Students consider the history behind several bizarre phenomena as told through myths or legends, then produce a myth or legend of their own.

## Objective(s):
- Define myth and legend.
- Participate in a round-robin myth and legend telling.
- Illustrate the tale.

## Materials Needed:
- pictures of an elephant, cheetah, and giraffe
- Rudyard Kipling's Just So Stories
- writing paper
- 1 copy of page 114 for each student
- chart paper
- drawing paper for each student

## Focus Web Site:
**Animals, Myths, and Legends**
http://www.ozemail.com.au/~oban/

**About this site:** This child-centered site will satisfy anyone's mythical wonder in one quick visit. Click the Legends link to select from a whole host of stories, myths and legends alike. Other links provide bountiful information and interactive play for children of all ages.

## Alternative Web Sites:
**Myths & Legends**
http://pubpages.unh.edu/~cbsiren/myth.html

**Legends and Myth in Cornwall**
http://www.connexions.co.uk/culture/index.htm

**Myths and Fables from Around the World**
http://www.afroam.org/children/myths/myths.html

## Pre-Internet Activity:
Display a picture of an elephant, cheetah, and giraffe. Have the students describe these animals and tell how they are unique from other animals. Ask the students to explain why the elephant has a trunk, the cheetah spots, and the giraffe a long neck. Then tell them that an author by the name of Rudyard Kipling wrote stories to explain how the elephant got its trunk, and the cheetah its spots. Share one of his myths with the class.

# MYTHS AND LEGENDS *(cont.)*

## Pre-Internet Activity: *(cont.)*

Explain that a myth is a story that tries to explain something in nature. Since these animals have strange features, his stories try to explain how they got them. After reading, as a class or in groups, have the students write a myth to explain how the giraffe got its long neck.

## Teaching the Lesson:

1. Review the definition of a myth. Compare this definition to a legend which also attempts to explain some past event but cannot be proven true. The two genres of literature are very similar in definition, so most stories that fall under either category are usually lumped together. Explain that the site the students will visit has a listing of both myths and legends but doesn't identify which is which.

2. Distribute a copy of the reproducible on page 114. Explain that as the students read one of the myths or legends, they will need to think about the story and decide whether they think it is a myth or legend.

3. Visit the Web site as a class, or allow students to visit it in groups. Individual groups may read different stories and compare notes after everyone has had a turn. As they read, students complete the work sheet.

4. After completing the Internet activity, have the students apply their sharp-witted story writing skills by participating in a round-robin myth and legend telling. Have the class sit in a circle. Begin the story with one of the titles below, or make up one of your own. Begin the story with an opening sentence. The first person in the circle must add to the story by contributing no more than one sentence. Then the next person adds a sentence, and so on, until everyone has had a turn. The class should understand that the tale must be completed by the time the storytelling reaches the last person in the circle.

5. Write down the students' sentences as they say them. Copy their story onto a chart. The next day, invite the class to reread their myth or legend. Provide drawing paper and crayons so that the students may illustrate their tale. Post both the story and illustrations in the hallway to share with everyone who walks by.

   **Sample story beginnings...**

   The Legend of [name of your school]

   Jenny and the Purple Frog

   The Missing Sock

   Mrs. Whettleworth's Dancing Pencils

   The Spotted Toadstool

# MYTHS AND LEGENDS *(cont.)*

## Extended Activities:

1. Mythical creatures abound in tales of fantasy. Some students may already be familiar with these creatures while others may not. Place the students into six groups. Write the following mythical creatures on note cards and distribute one to each group: Bigfoot, dragon, fairy, ghost, mermaid, werewolf. Working with their teams, the students list on the cards what they know about these creatures. (Students should include any and all ideas, regardless of whether their knowledge is fact or fiction, knowledge or speculation.) Allow time for the groups to share their cards. Explain that they will visit a Web site that lists these and many more mythical creatures with which the students may not be so familiar. Log on to one of the following Web sites, read up on the above-mentioned mythical creatures, and then try linking to some lesser-known beings. (Preview some creatures of interest prior to student interaction due to some graphic content.)

   **The Guide to Unbiological Species**
   http://www.gryphonheart.com/index.htm

   **Dragons & Mythical Creatures**
   http://www.geocities.com/Area51/Chamber/3105/

2. After reading up on the unexplained, have students create their very own mythical creatures. Prepare enough paper for each student ahead of time. Fold a sheet of drawing paper into thirds. Number each section on the top left side. Fold the paper so that only side 1 is showing. Each student begins by drawing a head in section one. Then they pass their paper with section 2 facing up to the person on their right (no peeking at side 1!). Now the students draw a body in section 2. They then pass the paper again to the right so that only side 3 is showing. (No peeking!) This time the students draw legs on section three. They pass their paper one more time. This is the one they get to keep. Students connect all the body parts and then color and name their creatures. If desired, have the students also create histories about their creatures similar to the ones read in the first extended activity above.

3. Is the class ready to take an online quiz? Most students are quite familiar with fairy and folk tales, perhaps even a legend or myth or two. But are they up to the ultimate challenge? Link to this site to take an online quiz regarding myths, legends, and fairy tales. Students will realize there's a whole genre of literature just waiting for them to discover!

   **Folktales Quiz**
   http://www.tiac.net/users/write/ftales/ftales.html

Name: _____

# THAT EXPLAINS IT!

**Find this Web site:** http://www.ozemail.com.au/~oban/

**Directions:** Click the **Legends** link. Click on a myth or legend you want to read. Read and think about the story and then write the answers on the lines.

Title of the story _____

Who was the main character in the story? _____

What was his or her attitude like at the beginning of the story? _____

_____

Describe how this character behaved.

1. _____
2. _____
3. _____

What happened to the character by the end of the story?

_____

What lesson did the character learn in the story? _____

_____

Do you think this story was a myth or a legend?

Why? _____

_____

_____

_____

_____

# JUST FOR FUN: STORIES ON THE WEB

## Description:

The Internet can provide a fun and motivating reading environment for even the most reluctant readers. The following activities allow students to discover the wonderful world of reading via stories on the Internet. Enjoy!

## Objective(s):

- Read stories online!

## Story Web Sites:

### Billy Bear Storybooks
http://www.billybear4kids.com/story/books.htm

Here is a short listing of stories young children are sure to find entertaining. Advanced young readers may read them independently while very young readers may need adult assistance.

### Candlelight Stories
http://www.CandlelightStories.com/candle.htm

No site holds a candle to the listing of online stories at this site! Titles include well-known fairy tales as well as original stories by various authors. The list is graphically motivating and includes numerous stories to choose from.

### The Moonlit Road
http://www.themoonlitroad.com/

Only go there if you dare! These interactive tales of the American south are ideal for lovers of mystery and intrigue but not for the weak at heart! The black background and eerie graphics only add to the magnificence of these tales on the Web. (Be prepared for extensive downloading time due to the advanced imagery.)

### Tales to Tell
http://www.thekids.com/kids/stories/

Select from one of four story topics: **Rhymes and Nonsense, Fables & Animal Stories, Stories from Everywhere, Heroes & Adventure**. There's even an FYI; read the histories of some titles or review a brief synopsis of what the story is about.

### Webtime Stories
http://www.kn.pacbell.com/wired/webtime/

This site provides an all-in-one listing of valuable reading resources for parents, teachers, and students. Select the **Stories** link to view a list of readable stories on the Net. Other links include **Games and Activities, Read Better, Reviews, Interactive Stories** (see page 107), **Resources, Recommended Reading**, and **What's Next?**

# JUST FOR FUN: STORIES ON THE WEB *(cont.)*

## Activities:

### On the Web Story Map

Give your student an opportunity to read a story found on one of the suggested Web sites. Use the reproducible story map on page 119 to help students organize information about the story they read on the Web. They may use the information they write as a reference for any one of the following activities, when appropriate.

### Vocabulary on the Web

Before your students begin to read a Web story, go over this activity with them. Students should always be on the lookout for new vocabulary to broaden their word knowledge. Copy page 120 onto various colors of construction or typing paper. Review the directions with the class and then allow students time to write unknown words as they read the unfamiliar passages. Afterwards, compile a list of "Web Words" to post on a bulletin board. Decorate the board to resemble a large spider web. The students may cut out their words to place on the board. Review the list on a daily or weekly basis, or conduct any one of your own personal favorite vocabulary activities when using the "Web Word" list.

### Logging Internet Stories

What better way to check students' comprehension and thoughts towards a story than to have them write in a personal literature response journal? Copy several pages of the response log and one cover from page 121 for each student. Staple them to make a journal booklet. As students finish reading a story on the Web, they respond in their journals. Once a week, ask for three or four volunteers to share their thoughts about a particular story on the World Wide Web. Do others in the class agree or disagree? Why?

### Predict Before You Click

Before reading a story as a class, review the story and gather appropriate vocabulary. Include numerous people, places, things, and verbs. Have the students use the words from the story to predict the events in the story by following a typical story map. Then go to the story on the Web and read to find out if the students' predictions were correct. The reproducible on page 122 may be copied onto an overhead for use with wipe-off markers, or provide a copy with the appropriate vocabulary for each student or for pairs of students to complete independently. Still another option is to list the words and have the students work together to categorize them in the proper columns. Then they share their predictions before going on the Net.

# JUST FOR FUN: STORIES ON THE WEB *(cont.)*

## Activities *(cont.)*

### A Reader's Theatre Encore Performance

Reader's theatre is a popular way to motivate students to "get into" a book. Students first form presentation groups (this may or may not directly reflect the number of characters in the story). Then they work as a team to rewrite the story into a script, practice their parts, and perform it for the class. For more information regarding this form of drama, visit the Web sites listed on page 140.

### An Online Field Trip

Move onto the Internet by providing students with an online field trip centered around a story's setting. Before beginning a new story, consider where the story takes place or its origins. Log on to your favorite search engine and find suitable sites to take the class to visit where they may learn more about that location. For example, when reading *One Morning in Maine,* find an interesting Web site about this far-reaching northern state. *Anansi the Spider* is a folk tale creature of Caribbean and previously African origins. Search and seek out some sites that share interesting information about this part of the world. Students are sure to take a keener interest in the settings of their stories with opportunities to explore the virtual world.

# JUST FOR FUN: STORIES ON THE WEB *(cont.)*

## Other ideas:

Students make a mobile of the characters or plot of a story.

Students make a poster on large paper or poster board advertising a particular story.

Students make bag or finger puppets of the characters of a story and then act out the story by using their props.

Students work in small groups to retell the story.

Students write or ask questions about a particular story to try to "stump the teacher" (or their classmates).

Students work in teams to write questions about the story and then use them in a storybook "quiz show." Each team takes turns asking another team its questions for points.

Nothing is quite as satisfying as turning the pages of a book to see what happens next. Work as a class to rewrite an online story. Assign a sentence to each student or pair of students to write and illustrate onto a large sheet of drawing paper. Combine the pages in sequential order to make a big book of the story on the Web.

Pairs of students work to provide an in-depth interview with the lead character of a story. They plan questions they would like to ask that character (and make up appropriate answers) as well as questions related to the story. (Ex: Wilbur, how did you feel when you won the special prize?) Then the partners conduct their interview for the class. Provide a play microphone, if possible.

Students make a bookmark from a sheet of 2 by 6 inch (5cm x 15cm) heavy tag board a bookmark related to the story.

Students design and create a wanted poster for the main character of a story.

## Your Own Personal Favorites: You Write 'Em In!

_____

_____

_____

_____

_____

Name _____

# ON THE WEB STORY MAP

**Directions:** After reading a story on the World Wide Web, complete this story map.

**Title** _____

**Author** _____

**Main Characters**

_____

_____

_____

_____

**Setting**

_____

_____

_____

**Problem**

_____

_____

_____

**Events**

1. _____
2. _____
3. _____

**Solution or Conclusion**

_____

_____

_____

Name _____

# WEB STORY WORDS

**Directions:** When you read a story on the Internet, write any words you do not know very well on the spiders. Find out the meanings of the words and practice them until they become familiar to you.

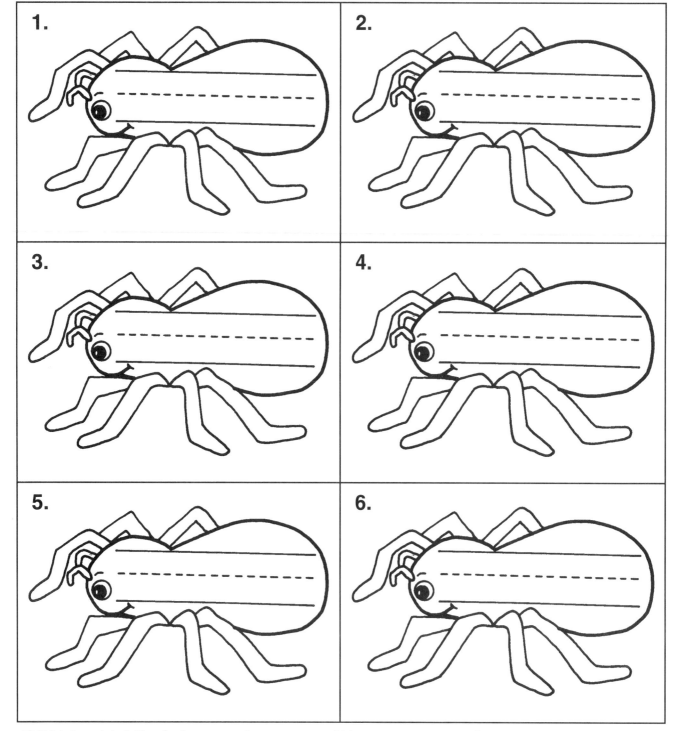

# WEB STORIES READING JOURNAL

_____'s

Title: _____

Author: _____

Characters: _____

_____

Setting: _____

_____

The problem in the story was _____

_____

_____

The problem was solved when _____

_____

_____

Some things that happened were _____

_____

_____

The character I liked best was _____

I liked this character because _____

_____

I would tell a friend
to read this story.          Yes          No

Draw a picture of your favorite part on the back of this page.

Name _____

# "NETTING" STORY PREDICTIONS

**Directions:** Use the words listed under each heading to predict what the story will be about. Then read the story on the Internet to see if you were correct.

Title _____

Author _____

| People | Places | Things | Actions |
|--------|--------|--------|---------|
| _____ | _____ | _____ | _____ |
| _____ | _____ | _____ | _____ |
| _____ | _____ | _____ | _____ |
| _____ | _____ | _____ | _____ |
| _____ | _____ | _____ | _____ |
| _____ | _____ | _____ | _____ |
| _____ | _____ | _____ | _____ |

I think this story will be about _____

_____

_____

I think this will happen in the beginning. _____

_____

_____

I think this will happen in the middle. _____

_____

_____

I think this will happen at the end. _____

_____

_____

My prediction was          correct.          somewhat correct.          incorrect.

# THE INTERNET AND POPULAR CHILDREN'S BOOKS

*Charlotte's Web* (Spiders)

*The Great Kapok Tree* (Rain Forests)

*The Polar Express* (Trains)

*Why Mosquitoes Buzz in People's Ears* (Africa)

# CHARLOTTE'S WEB (SPIDERS)

## Description:

Charlotte shares a lot of information about herself and her kind in the story. Students compare her facts to those online and then create a unique spider of their own.

## Objective(s):

- Develop a list of spider facts.

- Read about spiders on the Internet.

- Compare and contrast spider facts.

- Design and create a new kind of spider.

## Materials Needed:

- chart paper

- 1 copy of page 126 for each student

- miscellaneous art supplies: craft sticks, pipe cleaners, bathroom tissue tubes, cotton, construction paper, yarn, etc.

## Focus Web Site:

**Spiders Are Not Insects**
http://www.knowledgeadventure.com/encyclopedia/bug/rfispsta.html

**About this site:** From the *Knowledge Adventure Encyclopedia* comes this factual, easy-to-read site filled with general facts and information about spiders.

## Alternative Web Sites:

**The Amazing Arachnida: The Spider**
http://www.nwf.org/nwf/wlifweek/webspid.html

**Queensland Museum: Spiders**
http://www.Qmuseumqld.gov.au/nature/arachnids/arachnidswelcome.html

**Arthropod Museum**
http://www.vark.edu/depts/entomolo/museum/museum.html

## Pre-Internet Activity:

While reading Charlotte's Web, keep a running list of facts learned about spiders as students read them in the story. Charlotte was a common grey spider. Lead a discussion about other kinds of spiders the students may know about (e.g., black widow, brown recluse, tarantula, etc.). Ask if the statements on the chart apply to all spiders or just to Charlotte. Explain that to learn more, they will go online to a factual site about spiders.

# CHARLOTTE'S WEB (SPIDERS) *(cont.)*

## Teaching the Lesson:

1. Keeping the list from the pre-Internet activity within sight, go online to the focus Web site. Invite students to take turns reading the paragraphs about spiders. Each time a fact from the Internet matches one on the chart, draw a spider web by the statement on the chart.

2. Provide a copy of page 126 to each student. Allow students to reread the information from the Internet site, if necessary, to complete the page.

3. Knowing what they now know about spiders, have the students each work with a partner to design and create a new kind of spider by using miscellaneous art supplies. They should be sure their spiders match the true descriptions from the student activity page; no spiders should have three body parts, wings, etc. The students should also prepare a brief account telling the name of their new kind of spider, where it can be found, what it eats, and any other information they wish to share.

## Extended Activities:

1. Have the students work in teams to further research various types of spiders throughout the world. (The sites that follow are great Internet resources.) Students list five interesting facts to share about their spiders on note cards and then create a diorama of the spider in its natural habitat by using shoeboxes, yarn, construction paper, and other miscellaneous art supplies. They attach the fact cards to the backs of their projects. Display them in the library for others to enjoy.

   **Queensland Museum Explorer**
   http://www.Qmuseumqld.gov.au/nature/arachnids/arachnidswelcome.html

   **Spiders Are Fun, But Be Wary of Some**
   http://wildnetafrica.co.za/wildlifestuff/juniorpage/spiders/spiders.html

2. Don't miss out on these motivating, interactive activities provided by Disney specifically to accompany this classic novel.

   **Family.com Activities: *Charlotte's Web***
   http://family.disney.com/Categories/Activities/Features/family_0401_01/dony/donyout_nature/donyout049.html

Name _____

# ALL ABOUT SPIDERS

**Find this Web site:** http://www.knowledgeadventure.com/encyclopedia/bug/rfispsta.html

**Directions:** Read the information about spiders.  Read the sentences below.  Cut and paste the eight true statements written on the spider's legs onto the spider's body.

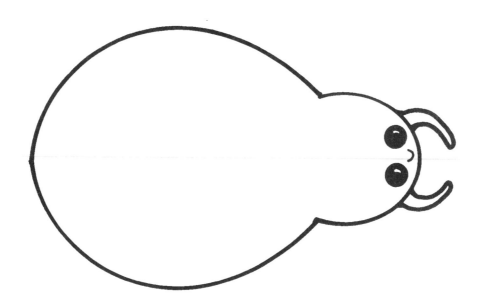

| | |
|---|---|
| 1. Spiders are arachnids. | 6. Spiders poison their prey. |
| 2. Spiders are insects. | 7. A spider's silk comes from its spinnerets. |
| 3. Spiders have no wings or antennae. | 8. Spiders spin cocoons. |
| 4. Spiders have two body parts. | 9. Little spiders are called spiderlings. |
| 5. Spiders have ten legs. | 10. Spiders shed their old skin. |

# THE GREAT KAPOK TREE (RAIN FORESTS)

## Description:

Students learn the true value of trees and their importance to the earth at a Web site that complements the information gathered from this story.

## Objective(s):

- Discuss the rain forest crisis
- List reasons why trees are necessary to the ecosystem.
- Write and illustrate an additional page to the story.

## Materials Needed:

- chart paper
- 1 copy of page 129 for each student
- drawing paper

## Focus Web Site:

**Tropical Forests**
http://www.seaworld.org/tropical_forests/tropicalfor.html

**About this site:** Developed by the people at Busch Gardens, this informational site offers students a chance to read brief summaries about Earth's precious resources. The first link, **Tropical Forests as Ecosystems**, provides all the necessary information to complete the student activity page. The remaining seven links offer additional food for thought regarding trees, deforestation, and conservation.

## Alternative Web Sites:

**The Jungle**
http://www.bcrescue.org/rainforests.html

**Toucan Sam's Rainforest Encyclopedia**
http://www.toucansam.com/

## Pre-Internet Activity:

After reading the story, create a list of reasons the animals used to persuade the man not to cut down their kapok tree. Discuss why the animals were so concerned that this one tree be left alone to live and thrive. Can one tree really make that much difference? Then tell the students that rain forests are disappearing at an alarming 50 to 75 million acres per year. That's about 100 to 150 acres each minute of every day! Explain that the animals in the story mentioned just a few reasons to leave the great kapok tree standing. They will learn more on the Internet.

# THE GREAT KAPOK TREE (RAIN FORESTS) *(cont.)*

## Teaching the Lesson:

1. Go online to the focus Web site. Connect to the first link, Tropical Forests as Ecosystems. Read and discuss the information here.

2. Distribute a copy of page 129 to each student. Students use the information on this Web page to complete the activity sheet.

3. Continue following the links to read and discuss additional reasons people take the rainforest crisis seriously. When finished, add new ideas to the chart begun during the pre-Internet activity.

4. Using all the valuable information they have learned about the importance of trees, have each student write and illustrate an additional page for the story as if they were the tree begging the man not to cut it down. Which reason would they give to persuade the man to second-guess himself? Combine the pages into one booklet entitled "The Great Kapok Tree Says...."

## Extended Activities:

1. Make vines by cutting strips of brown grocery bags and then twisting them and stapling the ends together. Have the students write one reason to save the rain forest trees on a leaf cut from a 9 x 12 inch (23 cm x 30 cm) sheet of green construction paper. Staple the students leaves to the vine and suspend it from the ceiling.

2. Students can take a virtual tour of the rainforest by visiting this site's "Jungle Journey." The images are breathtaking, and the information is worth a repeat trip! Other links include investigating some household products of rain forest origins, more detailed treks through specific parts of the forest, and ideas for teachers.

   **Rainforest Alliance**
   http://www.rainforest-alliance.org/

3. For rain forest research, this site can't be beaten. Each category (animals, people, and plants) is sub-divided for easy access and organization of topics.

   **Rainforest Workshop**
   http://kids.osd.wednet.edu/Marshall/rainforest_home_page.html

Name_____

# THE TREE OF LIFE

**Find this Web site:** http://www.seaworld.org/tropical_forests/tropicalfor.html

**Directions:** Read the information at the first link, **Tropical Forests as Ecosystems**. Then write the words next to their meanings.

---

### Rainforest Word Bank

| | | |
|---|---|---|
| oxygen | carbon dioxide | ecosystem |
| photosynthesis | food chain | habitat |

---

1. The complex interaction of plants, animals, and environment.

   _____

2. Plants are at the base of this. Without them, there would be no food.

   _____

3. With the help of the sun, plants make their own food by using carbon dioxide and water.

   _____

4. Plants also provide a place for animals to live.

   _____

5. This man breathes out

   _____

6. This tree gives off

   _____

**Bonus:** On the back of this paper, explain how the man and the tree need each other.

# THE POLAR EXPRESS (TRAINS)

## Description:
Use this story as an invitation to learn more about trains.

## Objective(s):
- Identify different types of train cars.
- Practice following directions.
- Cut and paste train pictures on a collage.

## Materials Needed:
- model train set (optional)
- 1 copy of page 132 for each student
- large sheet of drawing paper for each student

## Focus Web Site:
**Illinois Railway Museum**
http://www.irm.org/

About this site: Visitors to this site can access information about trains, the history of railway travel, and more. This site really has it all for train lovers and inquisitive minds alike.

## Alternative Web Sites:
**Railroad.net Yellow Pages**
http://www.railroad.net/yellow/

**The B & O Railroad Museum**
http://www.borail.org/

**Canadian Train Photographs**
http://www3.ns.sympatico.ca/othen/rrpics.htm

## Pre-Internet Activity:
If possible, bring in a model train set or invite the students to do so. Ask them what the purpose of trains is and why they think so many people collect model train sets as a hobby. Ask if anyone has ever gone on a train ride and ask them to describe their experience. Lead a discussion about why the students think trains are not as popular as a means of transportation as they used to be. Explain that people of long ago used to think a fast train was one that zoomed at 30 miles per hour! Today's bullet trains can safely travel 200 miles per hour. Tell the class that they will learn about the different types of train cars from visiting several Web sites.

# THE POLAR EXPRESS
# (TRAINS) *(cont.)*

## Teaching the Lesson:

1. Visit the focus Web site with the class. Click on the link to view the **Roster of Equipment.** Browse each of the different types of train cars: freight, steam locomotive, electric locomotive, and coach. (You will have to search for a listing of cabooses.) From each listing, select one of the cars that includes a photo, indicated by the photo following the name of the car. Take a look at several pictures of each type of car.

2. Distribute a copy of page 132 to each student. Have the students use the photos to help them identify each type of car on the student activity page. They follow the directions for each bolded word.

3. Ask the students what type of car they think the boy in the story used to travel to the North Pole. Does the locomotive on the cover look like a steam or electric one?

4. Using the activity sheet, the students cut out the pictures of each car and use them to create a train picture collage on large drawing paper. They may select either the steam or electric locomotive to place at the beginning of the train. They should also be sure to put the caboose at the end of the train.

## Extended Activities:

1. The Polar Express was so named because it traveled to the North Pole. Have students create a travel brochure for the [name of your town] Express.

2. The Polar Express took the children first through towns and villages, then forests, mountains, valleys, hills, plains, and the Great Polar Ice Cap. Have the students make a map to get from their hometown to the North Pole. They should include a map key to label each of the geographic regions above as well as the train's route to reach the ultimate destination.

3. Use the patterns on page 133 to encourage students to read, creating the "Literature Express." Every time a student reads a book, he or she completes the information on the coach. Display the students' cars around the room to make a long train. Use the engine and caboose patterns to begin and finish this ongoing project. How many cars long will the "Literature Express" become by the end of the school year?

Name _____

# ALL ABOARD!

**Directions:** After looking at some different types of train cars on the Internet, read the sentences and follow the directions.

1. Freight cars are sometimes called boxcars since they look like giant boxes and carry cargo.  Color the **freight car** blue.

2. Trains used to be powered by steam.  The steam locomotive held the train's steam engine.  Color the **steam locomotive** purple.

3. The caboose is the last of the long line of train cars.  Color the **caboose** red.

4. The **conductor** is the person who collects the tickets.  Draw a circle around him.

5. The coach is the passenger car.  Draw the faces of some people in the **coach**.

6. Today's trains are run by electricity.  Color the **electric locomotive** yellow.

# ALL ABOARD! *(cont.)*

Use these patterns with the third extended activity on page 131.

# WHY MOSQUITOES BUZZ IN PEOPLE'S EARS (AFRICA)

## Description:
Shed some light on the "Dark Continent" with these Internet activities and learn more about the place where animals mentioned in the story live.

## Objective(s):
- Study a map of Africa.
- Use facts on the Internet to answer questions.
- Gather three facts about a country in Africa.

## Materials Needed:
- note cards
- world map
- 1 copy of page 136 for each student
- poster paper or large drawing paper

## Focus Web Site:
**Kids Zone: Africa**
http://www.afroam.org/children/children.html

About this site: Especially designed to entice primary-aged children, this site boasts a wide variety of African learning from fun and games to literature and information.

## Alternative Web Sites:
**Africa Online**
http://www.africaonline.com/AfricaOnline/coverkids.html

**Africa Information Center**
http://www.hmnet.com/africa/1africa.html

## Pre-Internet Activity:
List on note cards the following animals mentioned in the story: mosquito, iguana, snake, rabbit, crow, monkey, owl, lion, antelope. Mix up the cards and distribute them to student volunteers. Reread the story and have the students line up at the front of the room in the order in which they were mentioned in the story. Invite the class members without cards to use the pictures to include any animals that are found in Africa but aren't mentioned in the story. Explain that these are just a few of the unique creatures found in Africa. Tell the class that they will have a chance to learn more about the continent of Africa online.

# WHY MOSQUITOES BUZZ IN PEOPLE'S EARS (AFRICA) *(cont.)*

## Teaching the Lesson:

1. Display a world map to show the students where the continent of Africa is located. Explain that a continent is a large land mass; there are seven in all on the Earth. (Review the continents, if desired.) Have the students make observations about the African continent.

2. Explain that the story originated in the western part of Africa. Focus the students' attention to this part of the continent. List some countries from the map within that region.

3. Distribute a copy of page 136 to each student. Go online to the focus Web site. Click on **Discover Africa**. Use the information found at this link to complete the student activity page.

4. Divide the class into groups of three or four. Each group selects a country within the African continent to research by using the active links from the "Discover Africa" page. Allow time for the groups to gather three facts about their country and make a travel poster with the information.

## Extended Activities:

1. Be sure to visit the **Myths and Fables** link from the focus Web site's home page. Many of the stories listed have African origins. Students may read one or two additional tales and compare them to *Why Mosquitoes Buzz in People's Ears*. Then they may write their own original stories following the same format.

2. Students may be interested in learning more about the animals of Africa. The following site provides interesting information for students.

   **African Wildlife Resource**
   http://www.awr.net/

3. Since the story originated in West Africa, be sure to visit this Web site filled with information about the world's largest desert.

   **Western Sahara**
   http://www.oneworld.org/guides/sahara/index.html

Name _____

# THE BUZZ FROM AFRICA

**Directions:** Use the compass rose to find and color the western part of Africa green. Read the information at the Web site to answer the questions.

1. From which country in Africa could the story *Why Mosquitoes Buzz in People's Ears* **not** have originated?

   Algeria          Ghana          Mali          Zambia

2. About how many countries the size of the  United States could fit in Africa?

   2          3          4

3. About how many different languages are spoken in Africa?

   100          1,000          10,000

# READING AND LANGUAGE ARTS TEACHER RESOURCES ON THE WEB

The Internet is filled with valuable resources for teachers and parents regarding reading and language arts. The following sites offer everything from book reviews and lesson plans to information regarding current trends and more. Whether you're looking for information or fresh ideas to try in class, don't miss out on visiting these sites!

## Places to Go with Kids

**CNN Interactive Learning Resources**
http://www.cnnsf.com/education/education.html

Read a featured story (abbreviated in the edited version for students) and engage students in the lessons provided. Each of the suggested lessons offers a selection of a wide range of reading skills. Be sure to check out the other links, too!

**Cyber-Seuss**
http://www.afn.org/~afn15301/drseuss.html

For every Seuss lover, this site is sure to please! Games, early writings, stories, quizzes, information, reviews...just too many links to list!

**Elementary Grammar**
http://vweb1.hiway.co.uk/ei/intro.html

Take students here to view a complete list of grammar skills. Click the topic to review the rules and see some examples.

**Grammar Lady**
http://www.grammarlady.com/

Four valuable, grammar-related links await visitors at this site. Choose the **Column** to read other people's most pressing grammar questions, the **Grammar Lady** to find out more about this site's creator, **English Grammar** to choose from a list of hot grammar topics you wish to know more about, or the **Grammar Hotline** where you may call (an 800 number) or post online your grammar questions. What an exciting place to hang out and brush up on grammar rules!

**Houghton Mifflin Educational Place**
http://www.eduplace.com/

Click the **Kids Clubhouse** link for onsite learning with students. Possible activities include reading ideas, games, and current events. There's even an online scavenger hunt! (from the **Fun Stuff** link)

# READING AND LANGUAGE ARTS TEACHER RESOURCES ON THE WEB *(cont.)*

## Places to Go with Kids *(cont.)*

### Index of School House Rock (Grammar)
http://www.yak.net/ian/SHR/Grammar/

Brought to you by Ian Cabell, download the words to America's most popular grammar tunes! (Sorry, no sound, but don't we all remember the music and chorus and forget the words to the songs?)

### Kiddie Lit on the Net
http://www.kn.pacbell.com/wired/KidLit/Kid.html

This site has a little bit of everything for everyone, including parents, teachers, and children. Choose from eight topics including stories, games, activities, book reviews, and articles for adults to help kids learn to read better.

### Kids Web: A WWW Digital Library for School Kids
http://www.npac.syr.edu/textbook/kidsweb/

Each topic of reference is divided into subject categories: arts (including language arts), sciences, social studies, and others. Within each subject category, students can search for the information they need on a variety of topics.

### Story Resources Available on the Web
http://www.cybernet.net/~sjohnson/stories/#forkids

From the table of contents, choose from a host of delightful story topics, including **Interactive Stories and Hyperfiction**—an excellent resource for online reading.

### Wild World of Words
http://www.enigmagraphics.com/stories/stories/forkids.htm

Click the **Wild World of Words** link to find some challenges students are sure to enjoy. Skills include spelling, decoding, word building, and word meanings. First, pick your skill within the language arts topic, and then the level of play. The true challenge comes from having to type in the correct answers—without a list from which to choose!

# READING AND LANGUAGE ARTS TEACHER RESOURCES ON THE WEB *(cont.)*

## Sites for Teachers

### Bantam Doubleday Dell Teacher's Resource Center

http://www.bdd.com/teachers/

Select the **Grade Index** from the "Teacher's Guides" topic heading. Here you'll find book reviews by grade level and teaching ideas to accompany the stories.

### Carol Hurst's Children's Literature Site

http://www.carolhurst.com/

From the "Children's Books" heading, select the **Grade Level** link from **All Reviewed Children's Books**. Choose your grade level and then the desired title to retrieve a book review and sample activities.

### Doucette Index for K–12 Teaching Ideas for Literature

http://www.educ.ucalgary.ca/litindex/

Type in a title, author and/or illustrator to retrieve a listing of possible book titles to review. Included, also, are suggested activities to try with each title.

### ERIC Clearinghouse on Reading, English, and Communication

http://www.indiana.edu/~eric_rec/

Here educators will find more information than they probably know what to do with. There's a question and answer link for teachers, lesson plans, hot links, and articles and information on a host of related subjects. Check it out!

### Houghton Mifflin Educational Place

http://www.eduplace.com/

Click the Teachers' Center link and then Reading/Language Arts Center to choose from a wide variety of reading and language arts resource pages. There's something here to suit every reading teacher's needs!

### Media Designs Educational Calendar

http://home.earthlink.net/~mediadesigns/Calendar.html

Holiday activities and celebrations will never be the same again! This home page lists several sites related to the days of each month throughout the year.

### The Purple Crayon

http://www.users.interport.net/~hdu/

Visit this site to read articles, get caught on new strategies and information, check out some book reviews, and more.

# READING AND LANGUAGE ARTS TEACHER RESOURCES ON THE WEB *(cont.)*

## Sites for Teachers *(cont.)*

**Reading Online**
http://www.readingonline.org

Here's a valuable electronic journal brought to you by the International Reading Association. Visit this site frequently to catch the latest in reading trends and ideas.

**Reading Rainbow Online**
http://www.pbs.org/readingrainbow/

Take a sneak peek at one of America's most popular learning programs. See what's coming up and investigate some sample lessons to accompany the shows.

**U.S. Department of Education Home Page**
http://www.ed.gov

Want to know what's up around the nation? Don't miss reviewing articles posted here. If you're looking for ideas, try linking to **Topics from A to Z** and then selecting the letter of the topic you have in mind (e.g., "R" for Reading or "W"for Writing).

## Reader's Theatre Internet Resources

**Aaron Shepard's RT Page**
http://www.aaronshep.com/rt/

For anyone interested in learning more about reader's theatre or looking for valuable ideas, look no further than this site! Included here are reader's theatre how-to's, scripts, and other resources. The following are two additional reader's theatre online resources.

> **Reader's Theater in Elementary Schools (Informational Site)**
> http://www.indiana.edu/~eric_rec/ieo/bibs/rdr-thea.html

> **Reader's Theatre Editions**
> http://www.aaronshep.com/rt/RTE.htm

Dear Parents,

We are fortunate to provide the most current electronic resources for our students. With your permission, our class will be exploring the Internet to gather valuable information related to various topics throughout the year. Please note that we will not be visiting "chat rooms." All of the Internet sites have been previewed and deemed suitable for young learners. Each Internet activity will be supervised by an adult. At no time will the students be allowed to have free access to the Internet.

Please sign this form to grant permission for your child to use Internet resources and return it to school. We welcome you to join us one day to experience this extraordinary opportunity (days and times to be determined). Thank you for supporting our efforts to provide the most exciting educational opportunity for our students!

Sincerely,

_____ I give my child, _____, permission to work on the Internet.

_____ I DO NOT wish my child to work on the Internet.

Signed:_____

# Congratulations!

## This Award Is to Certify That

_____

## Is an Internet Wizard!

Signed: _____

Date: _____

# GLOSSARY OF INTERNET TERMS

**chat**　　　　Live electronic typing conversation among a group of people

**domain**　　　Name of the server through which a Web site comes to the viewer

**e-mail**　　　Electronic messages sent and received across the Internet

**FAQ**　　　　Acronym for *Frequently Asked Questions*

**home page**　　First Web page for a particular Web site

**HTML**　　　Acronym for *Hypertext Markup Language*

**Internet**　　A resource of electronic networks used to provide information via an Internet service provider and Web browser

**ISP**　　　　The acronym for an *Internet Service Provider* (e.g., *America Online, Compuserve,* or local Internet access point)

**link**　　　　Point at which a viewer may jump from one Web page to another; may be within the same Web site or connect to a different Web site

**Log on**　　　The act of dialing into an ISP and gaining access to the Internet through a server

**modem**　　　Electronic equipment which allows the computer to access the Internet through a telephone line

**search engine**　Tool with which a viewer may search for Web sites about specific topics and/or information (e.g., *Yahoo, Infoseek, Alta Vista*)

**Server**　　　Specially networked computer that is always linked to the Internet

**URL**　　　　Acronym for a Web site's *Uniform Resource Locator;* think of this as the Web site's address; when typed in and searched, the Web browser takes the viewer directly to the site with this code

**Web Browser**　A computer program which allows the Internet user to view Web pages (e.g., *Netscape, Microsoft Internet Explorer*)

**Web Page**　　Specific page on the Internet

**Web Site**　　A group of related Web pages within a particular domain or access area

**WWW**　　　Acronym for the *World Wide Web*

# ANSWER KEY

## Page 17
bright-dull; light-dark
front-back; far-near
black-white; hot-cold

## Page 20
1. White House
2. White House, Washington, D.C.
3. Pennsylvania Avenue
4. Washington, D.C., United States America
5. Pentagon, Lincoln Memorial
6. William Henry Harrison
7. George Washington, Washington
8. John Adams,White House
9. White House, Presidential Palace, President's House, Executive Mansion
10. Theodore Roosevelt, White House

## Page 27
1. isn't; it's
2. They're
3. You'll
4. they'll
5. Don't; You'll
6. Doesn't
7. can't; They're; it's
8. I'd

## Page 30
1. January
2. February
3. March
4. April
5. May
6. June
7. July
8. August
9. September
10. October
11. November
12. December

## Page 34
turret, donjon, palisade,
garderobe, loophole, bastion

## Page 37
11 commas, 11 periods (answers may vary),
2 exclamation marks (answers may vary),
1 question mark, 1 apostrophe.

## Page 40
1. jump
2. odor
3. gaze
4. chubby
5. purchase
6. old
7. Search
8. Close
9. fast
10. Sick

## Page 50
1. Grandma, jjplease@littltykes.net, friendly
2. Jan. 12, 1998, cool toy, Little Toy Company, toys @littletoy.com, business

## Page 63
1. (n.) salesman
2. (adj.) having no value
3. (n.) sailing ship
4. (n.) food for animals or (v) rummage
5. (n.) mythical creature; half man, half horse
6. (n.) horse drawn carriage

## Page 67
1. D
2. J
3. E
4. A
5. H
6. I
7. B
8. K
9. C
10. L
11. F
12. G

## Page 72
1. jovial
2. furtive
3. nutritious
4. skirmish

## Page 78
pear; tree; me
hats; tails; pigs; rain

## Page 90
1. 2
2. 3
3. 1
4. 2
5. 1
6. 2
7. 1
8. 3
9. 4
10. 1
11. 1
12. 3
13. 2
14. 1
15. 2
16. 4
17. 4
18. 9
19  4
20. 6
21. 6

## Page 126
sentence numbers
1, 3, 4, 6, 7, 8, 9, 10

## Page 129
1. ecosystem
2. food chain
3. photosynthesis
4. habitat
5. carbon dioxide
6. oxygen

## Page 136
1. Zambia
2. 4
3. 1,000

# RESOURCES AND BIBLIOGRAPHY

**Software**

*Compton's Interactive Encyclopedia,* Version 4.0., 1996 Edition. (1995). Compton's New Media, Inc.

*Web Buddy,* Version 2.0, 1998 Edition. Dataviz, Inc.

**Online Services**

America Online (800) 827-6364

Compuserv (800) 848-8900

**Net Search Providers**

Alta Vista      http://www.altavista.com/

Excite          http://www.excite.com/

Infoseek        http://www.infoseek.com/

Yahoo!          http://www.yahoo.com

Yahooligans!  http://www.yahooligans.com

Hotbot          http://www.hotbot.com

**Literature**

Aardema, Verna. *Why Mosquitoes Buzz in People's Ears.* Dial Books for Young Readers, 1975.

Cherry, Lynne. *The Great Kapok Tree.* Harcourt Brace Jovanovich, publishers, 1990.

Classroom Connect. "*Copyright and the World Wide Web,*" pages 8-9. Volume 3, Number 5. February, 1997.

Gardner, Paul. *Internet for Teachers & Parents.* Teacher Created Materials, Inc., 1996.

Gleeson, Brian. *Anansi.* Rabbit Ears Books, 1992.

Haag, Tim. *Internet for Kids.* Teacher Created Materials, Inc., 1996.

Kipling, Rudyard. *Just So Stories.* Henry Holt and Company, 1987.

Mahy, Margaret. *17 Kings and 42 Elephants.* Dial Books for Young Readers, 1992.

McCloskey, Robert. *One Morning in Maine.* Viking Press, 1952.

PC Novice *Guide to the Web.* Peed Corporation, 1996.

Polly, Jean Armour. *The Internet Yellow Pages*: Special Edition. Osborne McGraw-Hill, 1996.

Van Allsburg, Chris. *The Polar Express.* Houghton Mifflin Company, 1985.

White, E. B. *Charlotte's Web.* Harper & Row, Publishers, 1952